CAMPAIGN FEVER

CAMPAIGN FEVER

The National Folk Festival, from
New Hampshire to November, 1964

Charles McDowell, Jr.

William Morrow and Company   New York 1965

For Ann
and Jenny, Will, Kate and their grandparents,
with thanks and cheers to the working press.

Contents

CAMPAIGN FEVER

New Hampshire

IF you want to see the beginning of it, you have to go where the snow is deep and the people are few and only a fool or a politician would expect to see the beginning of anything important. The custom, then, is to fly from Washington to Boston and, in Boston, to rent a car and seek out the road that follows the Merrimack River due north into snowy hills and unreality.

That way lie the beauty and the gentle madness of New Hampshire in the winter of its Presidential primary.

Here in New Hampshire, as if on a lark, begins the campaign that will continue through the spring and summer and into the fall, when an exhausted electorate will choose a President of the United States. It is the longest folk festival in the world.

The sense of unreality that pervades the New Hampshire primary is brought in mostly by strangers—wandering bands of visiting politicians, pundits, reporters, television crews, pollsters, pamphleteers, flacks and assorted camp followers— all charging across this charming landscape in search of votes, trends, significance and something bracing to drink.

Senator Barry Goldwater of Arizona and Governor Nelson Rockefeller of New York lead automobile caravans over icy roads into little Christmas-card villages resting peacefully under eighteen inches of snow. The crowds that turn out in places like Goffstown, Center Sandwich and Sunapee usually are smaller than the crowds that have come to shake their hands, take their pictures and read their minds.

Like a ghost, Harold Stassen stalks the state, advocating a federal subsidy for motherhood and reminding blinking natives that he stands at the "creative center" of American politics.

Senator Margaret Chase Smith of Maine, a frozen rose pinned to her overcoat, presents herself in a northern hamlet at dawn and stands under a streetlight insisting to a few incredulous early risers that she is running for President.

The agents of Richard M. Nixon infiltrate the countryside, passing the word that the Republican voters of New Hampshire should reject Goldwater, Rockefeller, Stassen and Mrs. Smith at one noble stroke by writing in the name of Nixon, the non-candidate who stands ready to save his party whenever duty calls. "I have not seen the Nixon agents, but I have seen their tracks," a Goldwater man says. "They are like Abominable Snowmen."

Voters receive mystical, patriotic letters from Massachusetts suggesting that the true salvation of the party and the country lies in South Vietnam with Ambassador Henry Cabot Lodge. His name would be as easy to write in as Nixon's, and more neighborly.

In Claremont, a little city of 13,000 at the foot of a swooping ski slope, the Hotel Moody gives a birthday party for its oldest resident, Miss Millie Avery, who is 90. As her eyes shine in the glow of the candles, who comes in to wish her a happy birthday but Barry Goldwater, all the way from Arizona. He is followed into the dining room by a large troop of newsmen. Microphones are hooked up. Blinding floodlights illuminate the scene. Three television networks and two wire services begin to photograph an old lady's birthday party. A score of expert political reporters crowds in close to catch every quote. Miss Avery, as it turns out, is not at all sure who Goldwater is but says he looks like a nice young man. A public-relations man from Chicago assures the press, however, that Miss Avery is for Goldwater.

Nelson Rockefeller marches at the head of his impressive entourage through the Cott Bottling Company in Manchester, shaking hands with workers and expressing intense interest in such matters as the conversion of dried raspberries into raspberry soda. Every worker in the plant, from Raspberry Soda to Tom Collins Mix, from Dietary Cola to Shampoo,[1] wears a big Rockefeller button. Is every one of them really for Rockefeller? "As a matter of fact," a union representative replies, "most of them are registered Democrats, but we want the Governor to feel welcome."

A West German television film crew, fresh from covering the Winter Olympics in the Tirolian Alps, joins Goldwater in the White Mountains. The Germans adapt quickly to the climate of American politics but are disappointed in the candidate's rather shy, staid and unathletic manner among the voters. The visitors take heart a couple of days later when they join Rockefeller and see him bound through a snowdrift after a voter, whack the fellow's back and whoop joyfully, "Hiya, I'm Nelson Rockefeller!" This is more in the Olympic tradition.

At the Hilltop Motel, a small establishment in the skiing

---

[1] Typical of the frustrations of political reporting on the run, you may learn more than you want to know about dried-raspberry conversion but nothing at all about the occurrence of shampoo in a soda-pop factory.

country near Newport, Mr. and Mrs. Raymond Murphy, the proprietors, receive a telephone call asking them to reserve two rooms for a brief rest stop by Goldwater and his traveling staff. The Murphys reserve the rooms and decide to serve Irish coffee to the candidate and his friends when they come in from a long day in ten-degree weather. Goldwater and his staff arrive on schedule, but nobody has warned the Murphys of the forty chilled and weary newsmen who invade their tiny lobby. There are only the two rooms available, but the Murphys turn over their adjacent home to the press for two hours and somehow come up with lifesaving Irish coffee for all. The Murphys, who are not even Republicans, are experiencing their first primary as new arrivals in New Hampshire, and already they are heroes.

Shivering in a camel's-hair coat, a genius in documentary television gazes moodily at ice fishermen's huts on Lake Winnipesaukee and wonders aloud why the natives would build a cluster of privies on a frozen lake.

A restaurant operator in the Lebanon neighborhood looks on placidly while Goldwater, a clutch of aides and a journalistic horde come into the restaurant at lunch hour. The visitors shuffle through the aisles among the booths and tables in a sort of snake dance, driving the waitresses before them and jostling diners' elbows while pictures are made of the candidate shaking the hands of startled people with their mouths full. When the strange, disruptive rite is over and the visitors depart, the restaurant man says, "Oh, nobody minds. Last week Rockefeller, this week Goldwater. At this time of year we are glad to have any entertainment we can get."

This kind of tolerant amusement is typical of the attitude of many of the citizens of New Hampshire toward their fabled primary. It enlivens a cold, dreary season every four years. Like the Dartmouth Winter Carnival, it is good public relations, a tourist attraction. But the New Hampshire primary is not taken terribly seriously as a political event in New Hampshire.

In the outside world, however, New Hampshire is treated as a political testing ground of vast significance. Allegedly, candidacies are made and broken here. At the very least, the voting here early in March is supposed to provide clear tips to the course of events in the primaries that follow in such states as Wisconsin, Illinois, Ohio, West Virginia, Oregon, Maryland and California—a total of eighteen preliminaries leading to the national conventions late in the summer. The communications industry, eager to start communicating political significance as soon as possible in a Presidential year, makes the New Hampshire primary important—no matter whether the local citizens think it amounts to a hill of beans. Nobody in the outside world is allowed to forget that Franklin D. Roosevelt in 1932, Dwight D. Eisenhower in 1952, and John F. Kennedy in 1960 got flying starts toward the Presidency by winning this primary. Of course, such champions of New Hampshire as Estes Kefauver, who won handily in 1952 and 1956, were less successful in the country at large.

The theory persists in political folklore that the voters of New Hampshire are a particularly formidable jury for an ambitious politician to come up against because they are flinty, puritanical Yankee farmers, strongly conservative and Republican, and instinctively suspicious of city fellers and angle players. This profile is mostly myth. Of the approximately 600,000 inhabitants of New Hampshire, only 10,000 are engaged in farming; by proportion of the population working in manufacturing, this is the second most highly industrialized state in the country. More than half the people live within fifty miles of Boston. One-fifth live in the cities of Manchester and Nashua. Two of every five New Hampshiremen are Roman Catholics. One of every six is French Canadian. As for politics, the tradition is Republican but the current governor is a Democrat. The state has no sales or income tax; government services are financed largely by "sin taxes" on tobacco, beer, liquor and horse-race betting. And speaking of angle playing, the most interesting thing on the ballot in March, so far as most New Hampshire voters are concerned, will be a proposition to establish the first state lottery in puritanical old New England or anywhere else in the United States.

About 100,000 Republicans are expected to vote in the Presidential primary on March 10. Their main choice is said to lie between Goldwater and Rockefeller, but they will be able to signify a preference, if they take it into their heads to do so, for Mrs. Smith or Stassen or to write in the name of Nixon or Lodge or the hero of their choice. Apart from psychological implications in the outside world, what is at stake is precisely 14 of the 1,308 delegates to the national convention in San Francisco in July. Democrats will come out to vote on March 10, too, but the lottery question is the main attraction for them. There is no opposition to President Lyndon B. Johnson on the Democratic side of the primary.

So here we are in New Hampshire in the middle of winter, wandering bands of outside observers stalking an amiable electorate whose most striking characteristic is its sense of wonder at all this imported excitement about politics.

I drove to Hanover in the northern latitudes near the Vermont border to intercept the Goldwater campaign party, which was reliably reported to be heading into the neighborhood the next day. After establishing a base camp in the Hanover Inn, adjacent to the Dartmouth College campus, I went out into the street to interview voters and find out what they were really thinking. That is what conscientious political reporters do these days: they try to find out what the voters are really thinking (and they curse Sam Lubell and the Alsop brothers for making a vogue of it).

Most of the people on the street, which was piled high with snow, seemed to be scholars carrying skis. Probably they were too young to vote, or not qualified to vote in New Hampshire if they were old enough; and anyway they were thinking about skiing. I passed them by. I was waiting for a truly typical elder New Hampshireman, a taciturn type like the ones in *Reader's Digest* fillers.

Soon enough my man came along. He was wearing a lumberjack shirt and jacket, heavy trousers and boots, and he had a ruddy face and sharp eyes and frost on his eyebrows. I stopped him on the sidewalk.

Yes, he said in the right accent; yes, he was interested in the primary. As a matter of fact, he was the majority leader of the Senate of New Hampshire and would be on the ballot as a Rockefeller delegate. My typical citizen turned out to be Robert S. Monahan, the college forester, who had been a student at Dartmouth with Rockefeller. Mr. Monahan also proved to be one of the least taciturn men in North America, and for half an hour he delivered the most enthusiastic Rockefeller-for-President speech I had ever heard.

After learning what Mr. Monahan was really thinking, I spent some time in drugstores, ski shops and blustery side streets trying to find out what other voters were really thinking. Everyone had a hospitable, helpful manner and gave the impression of talking freely, but I began to suspect that I was not finding out what anyone was really thinking. One of the winter sports of New Hampshire is not telling visitors how you are going to vote in the primary.

Back at the Hanover Inn, brooding over my notes while I waited for some colleagues who were out foraging for significance among the voters, I visualized a scene that soon seemed appallingly real to me. The scene was in the home of Harlow and Matilda Curlew, and Mr. Curlew was arriving home from his ski shop at the end of the day.

HARLOW: I'm home, Matilda.

MATILDA: Evening, Harlow. Have a good day?

HARLOW: An interesting day, I would say. I was polled twice, interviewed by four different newspapers, and interviewed on film by CBS.

MATILDA: Who were you for today, Harlow?

HARLOW: In the Gallup Poll I was for Rockefeller. In the Harris Poll I switched from Goldwater to Nixon. In two of the newspaper interviews I was for Mrs. Smith, but in the other two I had reservations about a woman President in these trying times. I gave CBS the old taciturn treatment, said nothing but "yep" and "nope" for three solid minutes. Wouldn't be surprised if I make the Cronkite show.

MATILDA: Harlow, you are a card. I was interviewed three times myself—twice here at home by door-to-door people and once in the checkout line at the supermarket—but no television. You know, dear, you've been on all three networks and I haven't been on television yet.

HARLOW: Now don't feel bad about that. You've been polled and interviewed more than any housewife on the block. And who else has been quoted as favoring two different candidates by two different columnists on the same day? As for television, I'm merely in the shop, where I'm handy to passing film crews.

MATILDA: And you sound so typical, too. You always have been good at that trick of talking with your teeth shut.

HARLOW: Quit envying my television career and tell me what you said you were really thinking today. Did a trend emerge, so to speak?

MATILDA: Not really. I was torn between Lodge and that Governor of Pennsylvania, Scranton, but I did tell the two newspapermen who rang the doorbell not to count Goldwater out. It seemed to confuse them agreeably. The AP interviewed me at the supermarket, and I said I was undecided but leaning to Stassen. I hadn't mentioned Stassen for a week, and it just didn't seem fair.

HARLOW: You sound like Fred Grommich down at the drugstore. Old Fred's been telling interviewers from the very first that he's all for Stassen. Fred says it's up to him to keep Stassen in contention.

MATILDA: Harlow, this whole thing worries me a little. I wonder sometimes if we aren't tampering with the future of the country.

HARLOW: It's a chance to have some fun, Matilda, and I say take advantage of it. I honestly believe I would feel the same way even if we weren't Democrats.

Senator Barry Morris Goldwater of Arizona, the living symbol of unadulterated, unhomogenized conservatism in American politics, landed at the little airport near Lebanon, New Hampshire, late in the morning of a cold, gray Tuesday to undertake another of his numerous campaign forays in the state. He had announced his candidacy for President on January 3 and quickly had taken a big lead in the first polls in New Hamphire. But now, even as he intensified his efforts in the state, Goldwater was slipping in the polls, although still leading.

A crowd of perhaps 100 rooters, mostly youngsters, and 25 or 30 news people met the plane. A smaller contingent of news people had managed to catch a ride from Washington on the plane. Goldwater waved from the door and helped his shy, attractive wife, Peggy, down the steps. He was wearing a black overcoat and she a red one. "Thank the lord," said a New Hampshire Republican functionary, "she's left the mink behind. She is a wonderful woman, and I'm sure she understood right away when they had to tell her that it never gets cold enough for a candidate's wife to wear a mink up here."

Goldwater shook hands with some of his greeters. He was soft-spoken, polite, almost formal; this remarkably mild-mannered man seemed somehow out of place among fans who so obviously regarded him as the boldest dragon slayer in the land. With apparent relief the Senator detached himself from a loud group of adult admirers and had a few quiet words with some Boy Scouts in the lee of the airport building. He told the scouts and their beaming scoutmaster that it was a good thing for youngsters to get interested in politics. He suspected, he said, that "you young people would do a better job in politics right now than us older ones."

Senator Norris Cotton of New Hampshire, the Goldwater campaign manager in the state, escorted the candidate and Mrs. Goldwater to a black Cadillac, which led a fifteen-car motorcade on a forty-five minute drive down the valley of the Connecticut River to Charlestown, where a public meeting was scheduled in the town hall at one P.M. Charlestown, population 2,500, turned out to be a grim old mill town somewhat softened by a foot and a half of snow. When the caravan stopped at the barnlike town hall, there was nobody to welcome the candidate. Even the advance man was missing. We were about forty-five minutes ahead of schedule because a handshaking visit to a mill had been canceled. The candidate did not enjoy handshaking in mills, and Rockefeller and Lodge were going to get the millworker vote anyway, assuming there was any Republican millworker vote.

The town hall appeared to be devoid of all life, but then three good ladies were discovered in a kitchen making sandwiches. The coffee was not ready yet. Goldwater stomped the snow off his galoshes and said hello to the ladies. Then he fell into conversation with several photographers on the subject of lenses. He enjoyed talking about lenses and cameras and deserted the subject regretfully when some reporters gathered around and insisted upon talking politics. A photographer asked the candidate to pose eating a sandwich, for some reason, and he began to eat one. Then one of the good ladies worried aloud about Goldwater having to eat a sandwich without anything to drink. "Get him some milk," she said with sudden inspiration, and the candidate was given a paper cup, which he drained obediently without betraying that it was coffee cream.

Standing in the big meeting room with forty reporters, photographers and radio and television people, Goldwater shifted the subject from politics by teasing two political writers from Washington about their awkwardness with a target pistol. They had been his house guests in Phoenix a week or two earlier, and he had outshot them consistently. Somebody made a bad joke about shooting from the hip, and the candidate laughed and started to talk about the techniques of western pistol shooting. Senator Cotton interrupted and led him off to meet some of the thirty or forty citizens of Charlestown who had arrived by now. Cotton asked the names of two likely-looking voters in fur-trimmed hunting caps and huge north-woods overcoats, and they identified themselves as members of the press from New York. "I can't tell the reporters from the New Hampshire people," Cotton said in his rumbling voice, "because the reporters look more like hicks than we do."

Finally Cotton escorted the candidate to the stage at the front of the room and introduced him to the small gathering as "a fighting, two-fisted American." Behind the tangled garden of microphones that had sprouted on the lectern, Goldwater spoke softly and casually about his family. His wife was known at home, he said, as Big Peggy and one of his two daughters as Little Peggy, he himself as Big Barry and one of his two sons as Little Barry. "Things get all mixed up in our

family. We Goldwaters have been mixed up for a long time,"
he said, grinning quickly at the press corps to show that he
knew exactly what he had said.

Goldwater made a speech that quickly rambled away from
a short prepared text and rarely returned. In the same bland,
unexcited way that he had told us about Big Peggy and Little
Peggy, the candidate said President Johnson was "afraid to
do what should be done" in South Vietnam and Cuba; the
candidate did not specify what should be done, but victory
was his object. He mentioned in passing that a recent statement on missiles by the Secretary of Defense, Robert
McNamara, was "the stupidest statement I ever heard from a
man in his position." Still there was not the faintest spark in
Goldwater's delivery, and I could not evade the impression
that he just was not much interested in his own speech. Then
he got himself into a little lecture on the effect of electro-
magnetic pulses on missile guidance systems, and suddenly
he was talking enthusiastically, and also knowledgeably, for
all I knew.

The first question from the audience after the speech was
on a subject he had not mentioned: Social Security. How did
he stand on it? Goldwater said he was glad to have the question because there had been a lot of confusion about how he
stood on Social Security. The main thing to get straight was
that he was not for canceling anyone's benefits, no matter
what his opponents said. He talked on for a while, gradually
shifting the subject to inflation, and he wound up on the side
of old people who deserved retirement benefits that had not
been chewed up by inflation.

Goldwater's problem in New Hampshire, and throughout
the country, for that matter, was demonstrated in his handling of the Social Security question. He was on the defensive. Similarly, he was on the defensive on the subjects of
control of nuclear weapons, military action against Cuba, and

American withdrawal from the United Nations. For years prior to the first primary in his campaign for President, Goldwater expressed strong and occasionally shifting views on the most provocative issues of his time. Probably no man in public life had put his opinions into the record with such candor or in such volume as Goldwater had in his books, his speeches, his newspaper column and endless interviews. His past statements were hung around his neck early in the action in New Hampshire, and the man who did more than any other to hang them there was Nelson Rockefeller.

Preparing for New Hampshire, Rockefeller's large and thorough staff did the research necessary to compile a symposium of the political views of Barry Goldwater. For example, the following statements on Social Security were a part of the record:

"Let welfare be a private concern." (*Conscience of a Conservative,* 1960.)

"The government takes six per cent of most payrolls in Social Security taxes and thus compels millions of individuals to postpone until later years the enjoyment of wealth they might otherwise enjoy today." (*Conscience of a Conservative,* 1960.)

"I'll say here that Social Security is a part of our American life. I wish that when they framed it they would have made it voluntary. If a man wants it, fine; if he doesn't, he doesn't have to take it." ("Face the Nation," CBS-TV, 1961.)

"I think that Social Security should be voluntary. This is the only definite position I have on it." (*New York Times Magazine,* 1963.)

"We would be a lot better off with a voluntary Social Security setup. . . . People can buy better protection privately than the Social Security law provides for them." (Philadelphia *Inquirer,* January 1964.)

Day after day as the campaign began, Rockefeller charged that Goldwater was an advocate of voluntary Social Security and that the voluntary system, by allowing the withdrawal of those best able to pay the tax, would wreck the entire program. In New Hampshire this caused great concern, as Goldwater's workers in the field were quick to report. He quit mentioning the voluntary system, but the issue would not go away. Rockefeller did not need new Goldwater statements; he was doing fine with the old ones. And Goldwater only reminded the voters of their doubts about him when he continued to defend himself as one who did not want to "wreck" Social Security or cut off anyone's pension. He found himself in roughly the same uncomfortable and uncharacteristic position—on the defensive—across a whole range of issues.

Sitting there in the drafty old town hall at Charlestown watching this likable, somewhat wistful and befuddled man defending himself, I got the idea that he was not having a good time and that he would gladly be done with the whole complicated business of running for President.

Before he left his Charlestown audience, however, Goldwater said, "On March tenth make your vote count. Don't waste it on somebody who's not going anywhere. And I can tell you, here's one fellow who's going all the way." Everyone understood that he was talking about Henry Cabot Lodge. The Goldwater camp was receiving increasingly unsettling reports about the quiet write-in campaign for the Ambassador to South Vietnam. Nothing seemed to be going right for Goldwater in New Hampshire. Rockefeller, the "liberal," actually was succeeding in embarrassing Goldwater by shooting at him with his own ammunition. And now Lodge, bitterly remembered by all true conservatives as the man who undermined Robert A. Taft in 1952, was threatening Goldwater from the political safety of a war zone in Southeast Asia.

From Charlestown the Goldwater caravan drove 12 miles to Claremont, an industrial town of 13,000 at the foot of a

municipal ski slope. At the insistence of Senator Cotton—
"Look, I have been in New Hampshire politics forever, and I
know what I'm talking about"—the candidate undertook a
traditional street tour, walking up and down the streets, in
and out of business places, shaking hands. The candidate
went through it gracefully but without zest, and he did not
cause much excitement in Claremont. I stopped to talk with
an elderly, sporty real-estate man named Merrill M. Dodge,
who had just shaken the hand of the Senator from Arizona.
"Nice fellow," Dodge said. "I was glad to meet him. I met
Rockefeller the other night after a banquet at the junior
high school. He made a good speech, and he also gave out a
recipe for fudge and made a nice impression. Mrs. Smith was
here recently, and I met her—a perfectly charming woman. I
met old Stassen right there in the crosswalk. He used to have
a lot on the ball but had it all whipped out of him. Yes, we
expect to meet the candidates personally up here. We want to
see what kind of people they are, but we don't get all excited
about it. There would be more interest in this thing, of
course, if it was an election for Governor or Congress or
something like that."

The big rally of the evening was at Newport, population
5,500, in the Mt. Sunapee skiing country. We stopped on the
outskirts of town for a two-hour rest period at a motel. The
candidate also had rested for a time at the Hotel Moody back
in Newport and, before that, had spent nearly an hour standing around, waiting for a crowd in the town hall at Charlestown. Those familiar with the hectic pace of the Rockefeller
campaign were astonished at such lackadaisical tourism.

Rallies were a specialty of the Goldwater campaign, and
this was an excellent example of the genre. The gymnasium
of Newport Junior High School contained more than 600
people, Goldwater volunteers from a considerable portion of
the state, eating a catered dinner under a cloud of balloons

hanging from the ceiling. The faithful wore Goldwater cowboy hats, sashes and buttons. Banners and slogans were displayed around the room. The head table, on stage, was decorated with candles and red, white and blue flowers that matched the flanking American flags. Two bands, the band of the junior high school and the Alpine Drum and Bugle Corps of Manchester, took turns blasting the audience. Led by the remarkably loud drummers and buglers, the candidate and the principal guests marched into the arena from the rear of the audience. A color guard carrying the flags of nation and state swung down the aisle, followed by the bands, playing "When the Saints Go Marching In" with stupendous power. A troop of Goldwater Girls cut capers in western outfits and white boots. Then came Senator Cotton, really marching, his head thrown back, his knees high. The candidate strolled along easily, looking around with interest, especially when he looked at Cotton. Goldwater smiled and lifted one hand for a quick wave. The audience whooped and stomped. The balloons showered down. When the candidate reached the stage, the whole company sang "God Bless America" and "America." The bands granted no peace while the head-table guests ate their dinner.

The program itself began with interminable introductions of members of the dinner committee, candidates for delegates and alternates, and leading Republicans from various noble counties of the noble Granite State. The television crews, perched on their platform in the middle of the festive crowd, had hoped to get a snatch of Goldwater's speech on film in time to catch a bus that would carry it to a plane that would carry it to another plane that would deliver it to New York for broadcast to the waiting world the next evening (instantaneous electronic communication, alas). The preliminaries went on so long that the bus left before the candidate was introduced.

Senator Cotton, who felt "hardly worthy of the honor," arose to make the introduction. He praised the candidate as "a true conservative and a true liberal," but he warned his fellow citizens that Rockefeller was trying to inundate New Hampshire and Goldwater in "a flood of money and literature and radio and television."

"Why, I can't even watch 'Gunsmoke' without seeing Rockefeller's face at the station breaks!" Cotton said.

Goldwater was wildly received. His signals for silence finally shushed the audience, and he began to speak. His delivery was by no means fiery, but almost everything he said was greeted by an ovation, and his spirits picked up visibly. He said President Johnson was a "radical" and the Republicans had a solemn duty to save the country from him. He went out of his way to mention Lodge, saying that he had "got things kind of balled up out there" in South Vietnam. After the speech, the first question from the audience was on Social Security. The staff was seeing to it, of course, that the question always was asked, the theory being that answering a question defensively was better than bringing up the subject defensively on your own. Goldwater said the Rockefeller camp was distorting his position, and then he tossed in as an afterthought, "When you have Jimmy Hoffa running your campaign for you, there's no telling what you'll say."

Later, when Goldwater was sitting in his car, waiting to be driven to Hanover for the night, Charles Mohr of *The New York Times* tapped on the frosty window and asked him what he had meant by the reference to Hoffa. Goldwater said he understood that Hoffa and the Teamsters Union were behind some television spots showing Rockefeller debating an empty chair (Goldwater having declined to debate Rockefeller). "There is a chicken roosting on the back of the chair with my head and glasses on," Goldwater said. "Yes, a chicken with my head and glasses on." Suddenly it struck him funny, and he grinned and shook his head as the car took him away into the night.

I rode the thirty-five miles to Hanover, over a twisting, plunging road coated with ice, in a rented car piloted by Roger Mudd of CBS News. The New Hampshire primary is, among its other claims to fame, a severe test of rent-a-car logistics and driving skill. The candidates provide press buses that stick religiously to the candidates, sometimes so religiously that reporters are left stranded in telephone booths all along the way. A car gives a visitor some control of his own destiny, the freedom to go exploring and find out what the natives are really thinking, and the ability to abandon one candidate and take off into the wilderness in search of another. It is customary for travelers to team up for company, economy and mutual comfort when lost. The word spreads fast when a driver "loses his nerve" on the wintry roads. When a driver loses his nerve he cannot be trusted at the wheel by his colleagues. He cannot keep up with the speeding motorcade. He will miss something important that a candidate says at Sugar Hill and then miss it again at Campton Hollow. He will jam on brakes when he sees one of New Hampshire's distinctive traffic-warning signs, "Frost Heaves," and be whacked from behind by a driver who has not lost his nerve. Sometimes when a driver loses his nerve he also loses his sense of direction and will take a wrong turn for Littleton and wind up in Franconia Notch. Walter Mears of the Associated Press once managed to deliver a carload of heavy-thinkers to deserted Hampton Beach beside the Atlantic Ocean on a freezing night when they were supposed to cover a Goldwater speech at Portsmouth, which lay some distance away on a course that Mears had missed by roughly ninety degrees.

Now Mears, demoted to the back seat, reminisced cheerfully about his lost reputation as a New Hampshire primary driver while Mudd kept the car rocketing between snow-banks toward Hanover. Mudd had not lost his nerve. He outmaneuvered Volkswagens on the ice, leaned into the turns, and sailed across the frost heaves—and he sustained a running, third-person commentary on his own driving as if he were announcing an Olympic bobsled run.

It was a stirring experience, but even so the Hanover Inn was a welcome sight. Although the candidate had gone to bed, most of the traveling party gathered in the tavern room of the inn for food and drink and a seminar on politics. This traditionally is how a campaign day ends, and this is the part of the day that often makes the rest of it seem worthwhile.

It was not long before Senator Cotton, a self-winding polit-ical lecturer of the Dirksen school, was speaking expansively of the good old days when a conservative like Barry Gold-water could take New Hampshire for granted. But not any more, not since the advent of a complicating influence on the politics of the state—the Democrats. These fellows posed a direct challenge to all that was right and proper, and indi-rectly they caused the Republicans to water down their con-servatism. With elaborate mock wistfulness, Cotton recalled the simple, happy time when Democrats were almost un-known in the north country. He told the story of a man in his eighties, a proud veteran of the Grand Army of the Republic, who was told that the Democrats were trying to get organized in his town and were, in fact, planning a parade that very day to stir up interest. The old man refused to take it seriously, saying he did not know of any Democrats in the town. Then, hearing the sound of martial music and cheer-ing, the old man went to the window and saw the Democrats' parade coming down the street. His face darkened, and he banged his cane on the floor and roared in outrage, "Why, the sons of bitches are carrying our flag!"

I left the Goldwater party mushing through the White Mountains and drove downstate to intercept the Rockefeller campaign at Manchester, the state's largest city (population 88,000) and home of the Manchester *Union Leader*, the state-wide newspaper that had welcomed Rockefeller to New Hampshire by calling him a "wife-swapper." Outwardly undismayed by relentless attacks in the *Union Leader* or by the evidence that this hysterical newspaper was giving bitter voice to a widespread unease about his candidacy, the Governor of New York was putting on what was in many ways the most impressive campaign effort in the history of this primary. To an itinerant from the Goldwater camp, joining Rockefeller was like joining the Yankees after a long interlude in the boondocks with a minor-league team.

The whole operation was fast-paced and smooth-working and was carried off with confident professionalism. The staff was large and efficient. Advance work was good at almost every stop on the itinerary. The candidate's speeches were pertinent and well manufactured, and he was delivering most of them with a certain force and charm. Money obviously was no problem, and no detail of advertising, publicity or political organization was being overlooked.

Apart from all that, if speed, bounce, endurance and good humor as a handshaker were what the people of New Hampshire wanted in a Presidential candidate, Nelson Aldrich Rockefeller was their man. He stormed joyfully through town halls and tea parties, hotels and hockey rinks, shaking hands and patting backs at a rate previously undreamed of. He did more than speak his famous line, "Hiya, I'm Nelson Rockefeller," and grin and shake the proffered hand. He had that rare quality that made it easy for him to establish some kind of instant communication—with one person in a mob— and he left the most dour voters smiling and speaking kindly of him, at least temporarily.

Rockefeller worked harder, kept at it longer and had much more fun than Goldwater. On my first day with him, Rockefeller hustled out of the Holiday Inn at Manchester after an early breakfast, bounded into his bus (where he always rode, in the front seat on the right, with his staff and the press contingent), and said to the driver, "Let's get going." In the next 15 hours, without respite, he marched through a bottling plant to shake hands with the workers; charmed a small group of women who had gathered to meet him in an ice-cream parlor; toured the adjoining creamery; walked up and down the aisles of a discount store greeting voters and then stood at the checkout counter to greet some of them again; stopped in a parking lot to electioneer, speaking French to solicit the votes of two men who replied in French that they lived in Quebec; toured three floors of the telephone company, talking mostly with women employees, who tended to giggle, but also getting involved in a 10-minute debate with an engineer who was emphatically, and resourcefully, for Goldwater; rode to the outlying town of Bedford for a luncheon at which he spoke to 180 people as a group and to most of them individually afterward; spoke to 250 people at a community center back in Manchester and had to be dragged away, still shaking hands, by his staff; ate dinner in a restaurant, having reserved a table at the door, where he could meet passers-by; invaded a private dining room and joined in the congratulations to a happy, astonished couple celebrating a wedding anniversary; walked several blocks, buttonholing voters in the street; spoke to 900 people at a rally and then stood in the only open exit shaking hands for an hour; hurried on to a French-Canadian club and made a speech in French and drank a glass of beer; and led his exhausted troop back to the motel just before midnight. As it happened, the last hand he shook that night, outside the motel, was the hand of a right-wing pamphleteer from New Orleans who had come to New Hampshire to help Barry Goldwater start saving the country from Nelson Rockefeller and the rest of the "no-win" candidates.[2]

As a matter of fact, Rockefeller and his staff had never been in much doubt that they could make a non-winner out of Goldwater in New Hampshire. They did not believe that Goldwater and his philosophy could stand a clear, hard test before a jury of eastern voters in the middle of the twentieth century. And they would give him a hard test. They would use Goldwater's own statements on issues like Social Security to support the suspicion that he stood foursquare for the repeal of all social progress since Hoover, or maybe McKinley. Drawing on the vast literature of old Goldwater statements, they would portray him as a hip-shooter, a man who would be impetuous in foreign affairs and reckless with nuclear weapons. Rockefeller's Goldwater would be a candid and honorable man who meant what he said—and what he said was appalling. From the first, then, the strategy of the Rockefeller campaign was to take advantage of the Goldwater "image" at its worst, crystallize it, document it, light it dramatically, and develop it as the villain of the piece.

Now, as the campaign progressed toward voting day, private polls and less occult reports from politicians in the field indicated that the strategy was working brilliantly, up to a point. A significant number of voters were backing away from Goldwater; he sensed to be headed for defeat in his

[2] The man from New Orleans, Kent H. Courtney, wrote in a special New Hampshire primary edition of his occasional newspaper, *The Independent American:* "Only Barry Goldwater has the ability to carry into both houses of Congress, on the wave of his victory, truly Conservative Republicans. . . . When the Republicans were under the management of Eastern International Liberals, such as Eisenhower and Nelson Rockefeller, the Republican party failed to attract enough votes to win elections."

first electoral test outside Arizona. But something was wrong. Rockefeller was not winning. The voters were wary of him, too, although they turned out to see him and smiled when he shook their hands.

It was a frustrating business. Although he was compaigning as a responsible budget-balancer in domestic affairs and taking a considerably harder line on foreign policy than he ascribed to President Johnson, it was possible that the voters could not get out of their minds an "image" of Nelson Rockefeller as some kind of wild liberal and dreamy one-worlder. Or it was possible, as an old man said in Manchester, that "he is too eager, that's all." More likely the all-important factor working against Rockefeller was the thing that many of the voters were talking about to each other when he was not shaking their hands: his divorce from his wife of thirty-two years and mother of his five children and his remarriage in 1963 to Mrs. Margaretta (Happy) Murphy, the mother of four. There was not much Rockefeller could do about the political effect of his remarriage beyond hoping it would simmer down as people got used to the idea. A conscious effort was made not to seem sensitive about it. The new Mrs. Rockefeller campaigned with him for a while. Now she was staying home in New York because she was pregnant, and twice a day the candidate interrupted his campaign rounds to talk to her by telephone (sometimes with news photographers shooting pictures through the glass panels of the telephone booth). A sixteen-page, Life-size campaign brochure, distributed to every registered Republican in New Hampshire, carried in its biographical section a snapshot of Rockefeller with his first wife in her wedding dress and another with his second wife after the remarriage. It is hard to say whether this frank treatment of the problem helped people to get used to the idea.

In any event, the Rockefeller candidacy was not catching fire in New Hampshire. He was cutting Goldwater down to size, all right, but the beneficiary of all this effort might well turn out to be Henry Cabot Lodge or Richard Nixon or some other noble soul who lurked above the battle.

By the first of March it was evident that Henry Cabot Lodge was going to foul up the Republican primary in New Hampshire, on the tenth day of the month, without setting foot in the snow.

"Foul up" was one of the more delicate phrases used by the Goldwater and Rockefeller staffs as they contemplated the probable effect of a surge of voter sentiment for the United States Ambassador to South Vietnam. Lodge was not a candidate, had taken no position on the issues, had shaken no hands. His supporters, in their wisdom, would have to write in his name, for it did not appear on the featured section of the ballot where voters would mark a preference among Goldwater, Rockefeller, Mrs. Smith and Stassen. True, the long list of local candidates for delegate to the Republican national convention included a slate favorable to Lodge, but hardly anyone even knew who these citizens were. Unlike Richard Nixon, whose write-in campaign was being promoted by a former governor, Wesley Powell, the remote Lodge did not have any of the well-known names of New Hampshire politics on his side.

The Lodge campaign—or "draft," as its promoters called it—was based in his home state of Massachusetts. A small group of eager beavers, former supporters of Lodge's son George in his unsuccessful bid for the Senate against Edward Kennedy, decided to cross the border into New Hampshire and see what they could do for the elder Lodge. It began as a small, ill-financed, unimpressive operation. This little Lodge cell, working in a room in Concord, managed a mailing to all registered Republicans and provided a reply coupon for those who wanted to encourage the Ambassador to come home and run for President. The way to encourage him was, of course, to see to it that a great many people wrote in his name on the popularity-contest section of the ballot and voted for the delegates favorable to him. When the replies began to roll in—thousands of them—the Lodge drafters were astonished and their man became a powerful non-candidate.

The significance of the Lodge boom was apparent to some people sooner than it was to others. One example of near-sightedness on the political scene was my own. I was still convinced after the middle of February that the battle was between Goldwater and Rockefeller and that nobody who was not spending large sums of money and rushing around shaking hands and making speeches could possibly win. It appeared to my eyes, which, admittedly, were not accustomed to the snow glare, that Rockefeller was catching and passing Goldwater in mid-February. A member of the Rockefeller staff, of all people, told me that this might be true except that Lodge was pulling votes in such numbers that Rockefeller's carefully plotted upset was turning into a nightmare. I would not have believed it from a Lodge man. Where were Lodge's buses, brass bands and girls in funny hats? How could he do any good in New Hampshire without getting his feet cold? How could he imagine winning without pumping every hand in Franconia Notch?

Rockefeller's and Goldwater's people were quick to appreciate the substance in the ghostly Lodge campaign. Private polls showed that his potential support exceeded that of either of them; the question was whether the voters felt strongly enough to take the trouble to write in his name on March 10. The Rockefeller people argued to the Lodge people—even argued through the static of the radiotelephone to the Embassy in Saigon—that Lodge should step aside for Rockefeller if the Goldwater conservatives were to be prevented from taking over the party. The Ambassador insisted that he was not a candidate and could take no part in politics; he could not even take enough of a part in politics to call off his supporters.

In the early days of March the Lodge volunteers, who had hit upon enough money to send out another of their statewide mailings, were saying that their man would come home and fight for the nomination if the voters of New Hampshire summoned him. Robert R. Mullen, a public-relations man who had assumed national direction of the Draft Lodge movement, said flatly that Lodge was an "active" (if silent and absent) candidate in New Hampshire. There were rumors everywhere that George Cabot Lodge, the son, was assuring people that his father was not just susceptible but downright hospitable to a draft.

Goldwater's last days in New Hampshire were dispirited. If he was going to lose, he seemed to be looking glumly toward bigger problems. In one of his last speeches, he bore down on a somber theme that he had not developed in any comprehensive way earlier in the campaign: morality.

"We now have a President who saves money by turning off the lights in the White House—even as he adds billions of dollars to our public debt," Goldwater said. "Why doesn't he turn on some lights? This nation badly needs them. Lights of moral leadership, lights of morality in high office, lights of conscience and honesty, lights of strength and courage at home and abroad. And lights of law and order! . . . Accuse me, if you will, of trying to simplify issues. I say that any man who stands for office has the responsibility to simplify and clarify. Confidence men use the tricks of complexity and doubletalk. Honest men do not. . . . I ask that your conscience guide your political decisions rather than your emotions, rather than slick tricks and slick shows. . . ."

Rockefeller campaigned doggedly in the last week, finding an increasing number of opportunities to reflect on the failures of American policy in South Vietnam, and continuing to warn urgently that Goldwater, here in New Hampshire, represented a minority of "extremists" trying to take over the Republican Party. From Rockefeller's point of view, the potential tragedy of New Hampshire was that the non-extremists, the moderate majority that he had tried to rally in one massive bloc against Goldwater, were being lured in all directions: toward Lodge in South Vietnam; toward Mrs. Smith, who had remained mostly in Washington, protecting some sort of ladylike perfect-attendance record in the Senate; toward Stassen, a haunting name from the past; toward Nixon, whose agents continued to leave their ominous tracks up and down the state while Nixon hovered elsewhere. Rockefeller was beset by a pack of ghosts—that's what they were.

It snowed in New Hampshire on March 10, 1964, but more than 90,000 Republicans accommodated the waiting world by going out and voting. Lodge received 33,000 write-in votes (36 per cent of the total), exceeding the wildest dreams of his backers, and won all 14 of the delegates. Goldwater received 20,700 votes (22 per cent), Rockefeller

18,000 (21 per cent), and Nixon 15,500 write-ins (17 per cent), and there was a smattering of votes for various others. The lottery proposition got the most enthusiastic endorsement of the day.

Although there was no contest on the Democratic ballot, Lyndon Baines Johnson received 29,300 write-ins as encouragement to be a candidate to succeed himself as President and Attorney General Robert F. Kennedy got 25,000 write-ins for Vice-President. This was a weird little byplay. The Attorney General's friends, hoping to help Mr. Johnson make up his mind about a running mate, drummed up a write-in campaign to demonstrate that sentiment for Kennedy could not be held in check. Lyndon Johnson not being the kind of man who likes to be so obviously nudged, this clumsy business obviously met with his considerable disfavor. Whereupon fast-working Democrats, including the chastened drummers-up for Kennedy, were at pains to deliver an even larger write-in vote for Mr. Johnson. The sad part of this for Kennedy rooters, at least for the more perceptive of them, was that they were left with the uneasy feeling that they probably had helped Mr. Johnson make up his mind about a running mate after all.

In any case, New Hampshire was a Republican show and the communications industry, which had helped put it on, concentrated on the Republican returns. Thanks to the thinking machinery employed by the television networks, Ambassador Lodge's victory was "projected" from a few returns in hand before seven-thirty P.M., when most of the television audience was just getting settled down after dinner for the year's first dramatic evening of vote counting. Alas, there was no drama—no seesaw battle, no tense waiting for the up-state vote to come in. Lodge had won. The machinery had spoken. Interpretation began immediately.

Everyone agreed that Lodge's blitz of write-in votes was a

stunning thing, but it stunned different interpreters in different ways. A Goldwater man said from New Hampshire that Lodge was a "regional figure" who could not win over the long haul. A Rockefeller man said that Goldwater had been stopped and that was what mattered. Louis Harris, the pollster, observed, "The more the declared candidates campaigned, the less votes they seemed to acquire." Chet Huntley said the returns seemed to indicate that the way to win in New Hampshire was to "stay 5,000 miles away and not upset the serenity of the New Hampshire citizenry." David Brinkley was absent and Huntley was handling wry comments as well as his regular duties. George Lodge said that his father's performance had been "incredible" and Draft Lodge movements would spring up everywhere. Eric Sevareid said that the whole thing had been incredible, and he hesitated to imagine what further marvels the future held. Governor Rockefeller took the most resourcefully optimistic view: "a victory of moderation . . . the voters have rejected extremism." Senator Goldwater, somehow more relaxed than anybody else, said, "I did something wrong. I goofed up some place." Then both Goldwater and Rockefeller went west to make speeches; they were both still running for President.

During the next couple of weeks, the most thoughtful political analysts in the country made a heroic effort to banish confusion and put the Republican situation into perspective. Goldwater, who had gone into New Hampshire with 60 per cent of the votes in the first tentative polling, had come out with 22 per cent. Most of the analysts just could not take Goldwater's chances seriously any more.[1] Rockefeller, of course, was out. As for Lodge . . . well, Lodge took too many

[1] Joseph Alsop, who had watched the campaign and seen the handwriting on the wall, wrote even before the voting in New Hampshire: "No serious Republican, even of the most Neanderthal type, any longer takes Goldwater seriously."

naps. Lodge's naps kept coming up in thoughtful circles. These snoozes, which he sometimes insisted upon in the afternoon when he should have been campaigning like crazy as the Vice-Presidential candidate in 1960, were recalled now to symbolize Lodge's ineffectiveness as a campaigner. The Chicago *Tribune* said Lodge was lackadaisical and inept. The *Tribune,* along with other conservatives, also could not forgive Lodge for the energetic and adept way in which he had, as General Eisenhower's convention campaign manager in 1952, torpedoed Senator Robert A. Taft's last bid for the Presidency. So Lodge was out. Mrs. Smith and Harold Stassen were out—had never been in. Governor Romney of Michigan was having trouble with his legislature, and was not much loved by conservatives, and was a Mormon, and seemed to be holding himself aloof from Presidential politics anyway. So that left Richard Milhous Nixon, the New York lawyer formerly of California, and William Warren Scranton, the Governor of Pennsylvania.

The trouble with Nixon was that he had been defeated for President in 1960 (and had not been entirely graceful about it), and then had been defeated for Governor of California (and had not been entirely graceful about it), and then had moved away from his "power base" in California—and, although he was a competent fellow with it all, the country was thought to be tired of Nixon. Certainly the analysts were tired of him.

To those who examined the Republican dilemma logically, the solution to it emerged with surprising clarity: Governor Scranton. Here was an attractive, rich, urbane man of forty-six, droll but not too droll, tall and fairly eloquent, who had been a whiz in big business and then a special assistant to the Secretary of State under Eisenhower for six years. He had been "drafted" for Congress and had won handily in 1960 and promptly had been "drafted" for Governor and had won handily in 1962. His staff made it perfectly plain to politically analytical visitors to the Pennsylvania capitol at Harrisburg that Scranton was merely biding his time and waiting for all the other Republican candidates for President to knock each other off. To political analysts who already had knocked them off, Scranton looked like the man.

There was a procession of writers to Harrisburg, and they produced a tremendous flow of newspaper and magazine articles, the burden of which was that William Scranton was a likely, if not *the* likely, Republican candidate for President. He insisted, droll fellow, that he would not be a candidate and that he was actively discouraging anyone from working in his behalf. He would accept a "sincere and honest draft" at the convention, but he could not conceive of such a thing. In interviews, Scranton had a way of changing the subject away from Presidential politics, and the analysts found the habit unsettling but not quite discouraging.

The fact remained that Scranton was not moving into the void created in the strange New Hampshire primary. What the Republicans seemed to have proved at the end of March was that they did not have a candidate for President who would be taken seriously. Surely that could not be right.

THE Republican plot in April would not have been acceptable for a Broadway musical comedy. It did not meet the minimum standards of believability.

Rockefeller was far and away the best organized of all the candidates and active non-candidates. To supply and support his excellent traveling staff, he had a headquarters in New York City with 111 full-time employees and bustling subheadquarters in Albany, Washington, Los Angeles, San Francisco and Portland, Oregon. As he undertook a massive campaign to win the primaries in Oregon and California, the Gallup Poll in early April showed that 6 per cent of the nation's Republicans wanted Rockefeller for President.

Goldwater had millions of superheated volunteers working for him in the fifty states, but they kept saying embarrassing things in their enthusiasm and one of the main problems of the Goldwater managers was to control the volunteers. Gallup found that 14 per cent of the nation's Republicans wanted Goldwater for President, which meant that his support did not go much beyond his workers.

Rockefeller welcomed Goldwater to the Oregon campaign by expressing his "great respect and admiration" for the Senator's willingness to let the voters see and hear him. Both Goldwater and Rockefeller denounced Lodge for hiding in South Vietnam and not coming home where the voters could see him and hear him and reject him.

Gallup discovered that 42 per cent of all Republicans preferred the phantom Lodge, whose people passed the word that he had no idea of coming home for quite a while. They moved a small staff into Oregon, purchased stacks of mailing lists at a penny a name, and pursued their ingenious campaign to nominate the Ambassador by mail order.

Goldwater said, "If the Lodge approach works, then I'll go to Tahiti and campaign."

Nixon did not settle for satirical remarks. He literally got out of the country—to South Vietnam, among other places, on a tour vaguely related, it was said, to his responsibilities as an attorney for the Pepsi-Cola Company. Nixon had 26 per cent support in the Gallup Poll, second to Lodge, and he meant to improve his position.

Scranton, 4 per cent in the Gallup Poll but the choice of the nation's political analysts, stayed home in Pennsylvania. He called a press conference, however, and the network crews and newspapermen swarmed into Harrisburg on the theory that the Governor finally was making his move. At the press conference Scranton said he merely wanted to "make one final effort . . . to get people to understand that I sincerely do not wish to run." While everyone was making a real effort to understand it, the Governor's friend Craig Truax, the Pennsylvania Republican State Chairman, issued a statement saying, "Twenty weeks from now we will be on the convention floor with Governor Scranton as Pennsylvania's favorite son." The timing of this statement a few minutes after the Governor's press conference caused some of the most thoughtful observers to give up trying to undertand the Scranton situation.

The Oregon primary, which would be held on May 15, was considered to have special importance because the names of all the leading contenders—Lodge, Nixon, Goldwater, Rockefeller, Scranton, Mrs. Smith—would be on the ballot together for the first time. (Oregon puts the big names on the ballot whether they like it or not.) Rockefeller and Goldwater campaigned actively in Oregon in April, although Goldwater cut back his schedule of appearances in what seemed to be a sort of halfhearted compromise with the theory that campaigning discouraged votes this year. The Lodge people opened local headquarters here and there in Oregon and optimistically hauled their mail sacks to the post office. The Nixon people worked in a low key, so that their man would not seem to have crossed the line from statesmanlike availability into crass eagerness.[1] Mrs. Smith sent word that she was a serious candidate. Only Scranton demonstrated a positive lack of interest, and there was no campaign at all for him. It looked as if he really was going to have to be dragged bodily into the arena after all the other contenders had battered each other into the ground.

While fans of politics tended to concentrate on developments in Oregon—and in California, where Goldwater and Rockefeller would compete head to head in June with nobody else on the ballot and no write-ins allowed—several states held primaries in April. Because of a variety of special circumstances, tactical ploys and convenient deals, none of these Republican contests provided a major confrontation that made for intensive newspaper coverage or colorful television shows. Wisconsin Republicans chose a delegation

[1] The American Society of Newspaper Editors took a poll of its members at its convention in Washington in April, and Nixon was picked as the probable winner.

pledged to Representative John W. Byrnes as a favorite son, but most of the chosen delegates were strong for Goldwater. In the Illinois primary, Goldwater received 63 per cent of the vote and Mrs. Smith, the only other candidate on the ballot, received 26 per cent; while many of the analysts were noting that this was a shockingly poor showing by Goldwater in the conservative Middle West, Goldwater was racking up another fifty or so convention votes. New Jersey chose an uncommitted delegation, but the Goldwater people said at least half of the forty delegates could hardly wait to vote for Goldwater. In the great majority of states relying on conventions rather than primaries to pick delegates, Goldwater was beginning to acquire votes as fast as all the other contenders combined. For a fellow who was sinking in the polls and campaigning raggedly, he was accumulating a remarkable amount of support for the nomination. On the other hand, there was no denying that Lodge won the primary in Massachusetts and Scranton won the primary in Pennsylvania.

The "image" of the Republican Party was much discussed during this spring of election year, and a surprising number of politicians were using the word right out in public. Nearly everyone had to agree that the "image" the Grand Old Party was projecting at this point was a muddled picture of mysterious maneuvering and bitter fighting on many fronts.

Meanwhile, back at the ranch, or at the White House, or inspecting poverty on a flying tour of six states, or wherever he was, Lyndon Baines Johnson, the thirty-sixth President of the United States, was the single "image" of the Democratic Party, and there had never been anything quite like him.

In the terrible period of shock and sorrow that followed the assassination of President John Fitzgerald Kennedy in Dallas on November 22, 1963, the country had distractedly accepted this tall, solemn-looking Texan and wished him well without much optimism and without having any immediate inclination to study him or speculate deeply on what kind of a President he would be. Now the stunned transition was past and the country was getting to know him as a President, a politician and a character in his own contemporary folklore.

He was everywhere. He was doing everything. He was unsettling and reassuring and petty and larger than life. He was the father of us all one minute and our slightly embarrassing rustic uncle the next. He ran the government of the United States as if he had invented it.

Johnson, the drawling Southerner, was pushing Congress to enact a stronger civil rights bill than many liberal Northerners had dared to hope for, and to pull it through the filibuster in the Senate he had put Hubert Horatio Humphrey, the liberal Democrat, and Everett McKinley Dirksen, the conservative Republican, in harness as a team. He was giving away big Texas hats to distinguished visitors at the White House. He was inviting tourists inside the gates to walk around the grounds with him. He had impressed a succession of skeptical diplomats with his apparent perception in foreign affairs. He had picked up a beagle by the ears in Washington and he had driven too fast, drinking beer out of a paper cup, at the LBJ Ranch in Texas. LBJ: those were the initials of the President, his wife, Lady Bird, and his daughters, Lynda Bird and Luci Baines. He had charmed the United States Chamber of Commerce, and he had announced a vast "war on poverty." He had cut the budget and he was cutting taxes. He had turned off the lights at the White House to dramatize the frugality of his administration. By his failure to be candid about his former Senate assistant, Bobby Baker, he had dramatized some of the dark corners of politics. He had settled the national railroad strike. He kept saying, "Come, let us reason together," and he kept getting people to do it.

He was on the telephone at all hours telling the Senate, the Pentagon, the White House groundskeepers and underlings in the Bureau of Indian Affairs how to handle their business. He was forever turning up on television in prime time to announce a disarmingly reasonable solution to a hard problem or to read a sugary letter from a little girl. Visitors to his office found that he had a remarkably sure and comprehensive grasp of his job, and visitors to his ranch found that he had the handprints of celebrities in the steppingstones and Muzak in a tree.

Although Johnson had been the dominant Democrat in Washington throughout the eight years of the Eisenhower administration and had not been entirely out of sight as Vice-President under Mr. Kennedy, the country was going through a period devoted to rediscovering the qualities of the man. Some liberals professed astonishment that the new President's program generally suited the liberal philosophy, particularly in matters of individual rights and welfare. Their astonishment abated when they recalled that he had been elected to Congress in 1937 as an enthusiastic Texas New Dealer and that Franklin D. Roosevelt was his tutor and hero from the first. "He was like a daddy to me": that was the way Johnson put it. Conservatives professed astonishment (and delight mixed with suspicion) that the old New Dealer wanted to reduce deficit spending, that he consulted Harry Byrd and big businessmen, that he was himself suspicious of some of the liberal dogma of the 1960's. When they had time to think about it, they may have recalled that the first objective of the New Deal had been to revive free enterprise and make it work, and that Johnson personally had been more than modestly successful in the wheeler-dealer free enterprise of Texas. And he had become famous in American politics, after all, as the Democratic leader in the Senate who advocated the middle road, progress through compromise, "the art of the possible."

The incredible Johnson energy, which now kept the attention of the country focused in wonder on the White House, had been just as incredible at the Capitol during those eight years when he was the leader of the Senate Democrats. He had worked fourteen and sixteen hours a day, running almost everything, arranging and rearranging, cajoling, persuading, compromising, and occasionally applying just the right political pressure at just the right time in just the right place to accomplish something that had seemed impossible. The high level of Johnson's competence across the whole range of politics and government was taken for granted in the Senate. Richard B. Russell of Georgia once said, "Lyndon Johnson hasn't got the best mind in the Senate. He isn't the best orator. He isn't the best parliamentarian. But he is the best combination of all those qualities." John F. Kennedy, among others, had said that Johnson was the best-prepared man in the country to be President.

While the Republicans indulged in the divisive exercise of trying to find a nominee for President, Johnson enjoyed the Presidency and the experience of being rediscovered by his countrymen. He liked to take his Washington friends and Cabinet members and reporters down to Texas, down to the banks of the Pedernales River where he was born in a small frame house in 1908, and show them the LBJ Ranch. He conducted tours, pointing out the cattle, and his airplane on its landing strip, and the white golf cart he used to get from the airstrip to the house, and the telephones hidden in crannies all over the place, and his and Lady Bird's twin white Lincolns with two-way radios, and the rain-water pools where catfish were raised for the table.

One night, with Douglas Kiker of the New York *Herald Tribune* and some others, the President went walking, carrying a flashlight and shining it around at items of interest. From time to time, other flashlights blinked in the quiet darkness—Secret Service men signaling their positions. The President crossed his own property line and walked up to the back door of the little frame house owned by his elderly cousin, Mrs. Oriole Bailey. He banged the screen door against the doorframe and shouted, "Oriole! Oriole!" Cousin Oriole was hard of hearing, the President explained.

She came to the door and invited the President and his friends inside, and they all chatted awhile in the living room, which contained two pictures of Mr. Johnson, one a portrait in color and the other a poster from his first campaign for the Senate, when his motto was "Roosevelt and Unity." The President pointed to a special telephone that connected Cousin Oriole's house to the White House switchboard. He made her laugh when he shouted to her, "Pick up that phone and Khrushchev might answer."

On these trips to the ranch, Johnson liked to talk about his beginnings, about his family, which had lived so long in rural Texas. His father and his grandfather had served in the Texas legislature. The grandfather was a Populist, and Lyndon Johnson thought of himself as a man who was carrying on that tradition of agrarian liberalism. Times had changed, life was more complicated, Cousin Oriole was plugged into the White House switchboard, but the main concern of politics was still the same: to make a better life for people. His relatives on his mother's side were Baptist preachers and educators. She was an elocution teacher. He grew up with old-fashioned, full-blown, fire-and-brimstone oratory ringing in his ears. His high-school grades were better than average, not spectacular, but Johnson became something of a boy-wonder debater and a declaimer who could rouse an audience of his elders at a Confederate reunion. Rather than going on to college as his parents had hoped, he

drifted off to California to make his fortune. When he became convinced that there was no fortune in picking fruit,
washing cars and digging ditches, he came back to Texas at
the age of eighteen and enrolled in Southwest Texas State
Teachers College. He earned money as a janitor and a gar-
dener and eventually at a job in the office of the college
president, who told him once, "I can hardly tell who's president here, you or me." After graduation—"I took forty
courses and got thirty-five A's"—he took a job teaching speech
at Sam Houston High School in Houston. Then in 1932 he
went to Washington to be secretary to Congressman Richard
Kleberg and he was caught up in politics as the Roosevelt era
began.

The President liked to sit in a rocker at the ranch and
reminisce about the old days, but he did not seem to be
completely happy unless he could step into the next room
now and again, sit down with a clutch of aides who had flown
in from Washington, and pass some miracle of state in time
for the morning papers. Then he would lead the visitors out
to look at his bulls and perhaps to hear one of his favorite
stories, the one about Magnus Johnson, the Minnesota Congressman who got carried away in debate and bellowed to the
House, "The only thing to do is grab the bull by the tail and
look the situation in the face."

Johnson was not as relaxed in Washington as he was at the
ranch, but he was having a good spring in Congress and in
the public opinion polls and he was enjoying the job. Speaking to the United States Chamber of Commerce in April, he
said, "I do not accept the viewpoint that business and government are inherently hostile opponents. . . . But I must
apologize to you this morning—we haven't done anything for
business this week. But please remember this is only Monday
morning." Aware that he was known as a man with a very
thin skin and also that stories of his fast driving and beer

drinking at the ranch had given rise to some editorial-page outrage, the President told the big businessmen, "If any of you show up at the LBJ ranch, we have some new rules. Everybody is going to walk from now on, and I am going to do what Lady Bird tells me. And we are going to make everybody drink nothing but pure rain water or Pepsi-Cola."

He was still refusing to admit that he would be a candidate for President in the fall and declining to discuss politics in detail, but he did tell a group of editors and publishers, "I think that it is very important that we have a two-party country. I am a fellow that likes small parties, and the Republican Party is about the size I like."

Most of the President's public statements, especially those made in formal situations, bore the marks of all those rural politicians, preachers and elocutionists in his background. For ears accustomed to the dry, sophisticated eloquence of John F. Kennedy, this man was too southern, too fatherly, too calculating, too full of sentimental gas, boosterism, exhortation and something wonderful for everybody who follows the golden rule and heeds the word of LBJ. It became fashionable among the liberal cultists and the far-right pamphleteers, almost simultaneously, to refer to the President as "Ol' Cornpone."

The American people had not been exposed to a southern politician as President since Andrew Johnson had succeeded Abraham Lincoln in 1865. To appreciate Lyndon Johnson and his talents without being distracted by the cornpone factor, it probably was helpful to have had some experience with southern politicians in their native habitat. Tom Wicker of *The New York Times,* who had lived among southern politicians for years before he began covering Johnson in the Senate and the White House, offered this assessment of the President: "Mr. Johnson is essentially an evangelist in the White House . . . an old-fashioned circuit-rider who considers the nation his flock and fears not at all to preach fire and brimstone if the call to the altar fails. . . . Cornpone it may be . . . but so long as Lyndon Johnson's evangelism comes from the heart, the nation is likely to get the message more often than not."

Uncharitable Republicans said, of course, that Johnson was just putting on a show. In any case, he looked like a hard man to upstage.

There was a side show that bore watching during this political springtime when so many strange and wondrous things were stirring restlessly in the land. George C. Wallace, the Governor of Alabama, came up out of the South to campaign in the Democratic primaries in Wisconsin, Indiana and Maryland. He was a chunky, neat little man with an Elvis Presley haircut and quick eyes and a dimple in his chin, and he carried himself like a middleweight boxer. It was possible to imagine that he rode around on a motorcycle, but the truth was the he rode around in the back seat of a big black car between bodyguards and that he was a man of considerable stature in rebellious southern circles.

Wallace had "stood in the schoolhouse door" in an attempt to prevent the desegregation of the University of Alabama in 1963. He had stepped aside in the end, but he had stood there long enough to solidify himself as a symbol. Now he was ostensibly a candidate for President of the United States, and he was campaigning frankly in the North as a segregationist and a states'-rights conservative. He was just a racist in the eyes of many, but, as he liked to say, at least he wasn't a hypocrite about it.

He said that the North was full of hypocrites who talked piously about the rights of Negroes while discriminating against the Negroes at every turn, and that Negroes were far better off among their friends in the South. Wallace had entered the primaries as a service to northern non-hypocrites, or maybe to northern hypocrites—some people could not get that straight, but probably it did not matter. What did matter was that Democrats outside the South could go into a voting booth and express their opposition to the civil rights bill pending in the Senate and to the Negro rights movement generally.

Wallace said the whole country would rise up against the civil rights bill "when people outside the South, who thought it was only directed against us heathens in Alabama and Mississippi, realize that it's against them, too."

In the Wisconsin Democratic primary early in April, Wallace received about 265,000 votes (34 per cent of the total), against about 510,000 for Governor John W. Reynolds, who was running as a stand-in for President Johnson. It was a very strong showing by the southern segregationist. "Backlash" suddenly became the most discussed political phenomenon of the time. If Wallace's vote was any measure of northern white resentment of Negro advances, the political consequences, not to mention the social consequences, could be enormous. Barry Goldwater's stock went up; maybe his "constitutional conservatism" on civil rights was sound politics after all. President Johnson was concerned—not as concerned as a few of his friends, who showed signs of imminent panic, but concerned.

Wallace, elated, hastened to carry his message to Indiana and Maryland, both of which would have primaries in May. He was a good campaigner, in his way, and he was received enthusiastically by audiences that sometimes were surprisingly large. Some of these people who turned out to whoop it up for Wallace were youngsters in leather jackets, but more of them were severely well-dressed, solemn-looking, mature citizens. They nodded grimly and they clapped hard. The more sophisticated of them felt the need to reassure each other that this man from Alabama was not of the common run of red-neck rabble rousers. He spoke out for conservatism, states' rights and segregation, but he did not yell or wave his arms or snap his galluses . . . now did he?

No, he did not. He always spoke in a well-modulated voice and was most restrained in his gestures when he said, "I hate to be so crude, but we've got a sorry, no-account, lousy federal court system in this country."

In a typical speech Wallace mentioned that he was "sick, tired, disturbed and fed up with a government that tramples its people and kowtows to its enemies." He suspected that millions of patriots were as fed up as he was with "ivory tower social engineers in Washington, D.C. . . . the Warren, left-wing court . . . and the left-wing press.[2]

Members of his audiences and of the press often asked the Governor of Alabama if he didn't think he and Barry Goldwater agreed on most issues. And didn't he think his presence in the race for President would hurt Goldwater? Wallace replied that he wanted to see whom the Republicans nominated and what sort of platform they wrote before he answered questions like that. "You know, they may take the South for granted and shimmy around with the liberals. How do we know?" he said. He said he would be "a most happy man" if a candidate on one of the national tickets ran on a states'-rights platform, and the implication was that he would withdraw from the scene in that event. For the present, he said, "Let's don't let 'em know what we're going to do. Let 'em pay some attention to us. Let 'em put up or shut up!"

Some of the Goldwater Republicans were paying very close attention indeed to this Alabama statesmanship. With south-

[2] Wallace always got a big laugh, followed by applause, when he identified several "magazines for left-wingers": *"Time* and *Newsweek* for those who can't think, *Life* and *Look* for those who can't read, the *Saturday Evening Post* for those who can't read or think."

ern Democrats like Wallace (and weren't they all?) in a more desperate mood than usual about civil rights, and with northern Democrats doing all this encouraging backlashing, the case was stronger than ever for the Republicans to quit shimmying around with the liberals.

It was widely assumed that the Wallace campaign was an embarrassment, at best, to President Johnson. For optimistic Democrats, however, there was another way to look at it. If the big urban voting blocs of the North needed a dramatic demonstration of the difference between this new, drawling southern President and the George Wallaces of the South; if the racist overtones of the Wallace adventure had the effect of cheapening the Constitutional arguments against parts of the civil rights bill; if the President preferred Goldwater as the easiest man to beat among the Republican contenders; if all this was true, then Wallace and the Republicans who thought they were learning something from him were playing into Mr. Johnson's hands. They were throwing him into the brier patch, which, as readers of Uncle Remus would have known, was where he wanted to be.

California

At 4848 Wilshire Boulevard in Los Angeles, on an island of palms and green lawns not yet captured by shiny new glass office buildings, stood a run-down, pseudo-Spanish mansion, vintage 1927. On the roof of faded-orange tile there was a huge sign saying, "Goldwater—A Choice Not An Echo."

This was the state headquarters of Senator Goldwater's campaign in the California Republican Presidential primary —the "critical," the "crucial," the "climactic" California primary, as the experts kept calling it. This would be the last of the series of preconvention tests. What had begun in the craggy, snowy unreality of New Hampshire would end in the soft and sunny unreality of California.

The rented house on Wilshire Boulevard was filled with enthusiasm, anachronism and perhaps deceptively amateur-ish confusion. The house must have been a show place in its day. Beyond the heavy, elaborately carved front door was a vaulted entrance hall with a marble floor. Under a tremendous chandelier sat a receptionist at a temporary switchboard. Again and again she said, "Goldwater for President, Goldwater for President, Goldwater for President," and her shrill voice tinkled the chandelier, or maybe I imagined it.

Behind the receptionist, in what must have been the dining room, several young volunteers were stuffing campaign materials into boxes and envelopes for mailing to the faithful throughout California. Bumper stickers were the big item— bumper stickers that said Goldwater in a dozen different slogans, bumper stickers that said Goldwater in Spanish and French and Chinese, bumper stickers that said Au H_2O. The Senator was till losing in the public opinion polls, but he was winning big on the bumpers of America, and these people were pressing their advantage. With all the bumper stickers, the room was dominated by a portrait on the wall, a glowingly bad and heroic oil portrait of Barry Goldwater. He had a gold halo.

A likable, philosophical professional named Burt Leiper, who worked for Baus and Ross, campaign consultants, took me on a tour of the headquarters. Rolling his eyes at the portrait, he said, "Volunteers may try your patience some of the time, most of the time, with an excess of zeal—we are having a run of portraits right now—but these volunteers will work. We are depending on them to win this thing for us."

There were tens of thousands of eager Goldwater volunteers in California, comparatively few of them portrait painters, and the professional staff knew how to use them to distribute literature, conduct door-to-door interviews, compile reports on those canvasses, go back to each door again to work on the "undecideds" and "probables," organize coffees, and yell at rallies. For the first time that many professionals could remember, there were actually more volunteers than were needed in a political campaign. Committees of them were put to work thinking up make-work for some of the others.

As Leiper led the way through the busy rooms of the old house, I heard the same curious-sounding suggestion from grinning college-age workers in both the parlor and the library: "Show him the bathroom." There were several, but the one they were talking about was on the second floor. It was a cavern in shocking-pink tile, featuring a steam room with bas-relief heads of noble Romans, a shower with nozzles at all angles and levels, and a splendid sunken tub. This magnificent chamber was being used for the mimeographing of press releases. A television cameraman from the British Broadcasting Company was measuring the room for camera angles preparatory to memorializing it on film for our British cousins, who already had enough trouble understanding American politics—and now this.

Leiper and I left the BBC man there in the bathroom, humming with delight, and went up to the sunroom on the roof, headquarters of Youth for Goldwater. The youth were in school at the time, happily enough, and there was not much to see except an array of posters bearing such slogans as "U.S. Needs Gold and Water to Stay Solvent." Leiper pointed out the posters wordlessly, but he was a good wincer.

Back downstairs we looked in briefly on a couple of professionals working on the telephone, lining up television time and trying to "co-ordinate plans" with various members of the campaign hierarchy, which included former Senator William F. Knowland, the state manager; the regular Republican organization; the more or less independent Goldwater for President clubs and various exotic satellites of California Republicanism; the campaign consultants, who concentrated on public relations and advertising, but also got involved in political organization; and Senator Goldwater's national campaign staff. I moved on down the hall to the water cooler, where several volunteers were gathered. A young man opened the refrigerated compartment under the water spout and produced what at first appeared to be several cans of cold beer. But, no, the cans were labeled "Gold Water, the Right Drink for the Conservative Taste."

We all had a drink, and it wasn't bad on a hot day if you liked the taste of something like 7-Up combined with something like weak orangeade. The young volunteers were friendly, high-spirited and optimistic. They were flatly certain that Senator Goldwater would win the primary and would be nominated for President. I mentioned a poll that showed Rockefeller running slightly ahead of Goldwater in California, and the volunteers laughed—genuine laughter, not forced—and said the poll was crazy. A young woman said she was not as sure as the others seemed to be that the poll was crazy, but she hoped it was, because Barry Goldwater was the last chance to save America. After that there was a lull in the conversation and somebody said, "Well, back to work, then."

The young woman who had been so serious about saving America managed a smile, went to a desk, opened a drawer and made me a present of a bottle labeled "Gold Water, An After-Shave for Americans."

In the merry month of May the candidates and their staffs, the reporters, pundits, pollsters and television crews migrated to the West for the big show in California—voting day would be June 2—and the warm-up event in Oregon on May 15. Meanwhile, during the first two weeks of the month, events of less dramatic value but much political importance were taking place all over the country.

The Republicans of Texas, though not required by law or custom to hold a Presidential primary, put one on anyway, just to demonstrate how badly Barry Goldwater could beat

Nelson Rockefeller. Goldwater cornered the fifty-six convention votes of Texas. The Republicans of Indiana held a primary and voted three to one for Goldwater over Stassen, the only other name on the ballot; all experts agreed that this was a poor showing by Goldwater against a token candidate, but the thiry-two delegates were pledged to Goldwater. He accumulated more delegates in primaries and conventions in Wyoming, Nebraska, West Virginia and Rhode Island. Michigan Republicans were lining up peacefully behind Governor George Romney as a favorite son, but many of the delegates in the line were known to be hard-rock Goldwater people who had been prevailed upon by the Senator's strategists to play it cool for the time being. Goldwater spoke at the Georgia Republican convention in Atlanta and departed with twenty-two of twenty-four delegates pledged to him. The Tennessee convention endorsed him by resolution. He was picking up delegates in Congressional district conventions that preceded state conventions, and then he was picking up at-large delegates elected by the conventions themselves. Alabama, Arkansas, Florida, Louisiana, Mississippi, North Carolina, South Carolina, Oklahoma and Virginia were almost solid for Goldwater. The precisely planned Goldwater drive in the South, directed by a thirty-three-year-old Alabama lawyer named John Grenier, went back more than two years to the time when Goldwater people began working methodically at the town and county levels to deliver these delegate votes in 1964. The delivery was not as massive outside the South, but Goldwater was gaining a vote here, a vote there, seven in one state, fourteen in another, and they all added up.[1]

---

[1] The student mock convention at Washington and Lee University, Lexington, Virginia, which had in the past correctly picked 8 of 12 nominees of the party out of power, chose Goldwater on the second ballot (he had 601 votes on the first). Of all collegiate mock conventions, this one puts most emphasis on "scientific method." Questionnaires were sent

Quite suddenly, in the early days of May, the newspapers, magazines and networks looked away from the polls and the campaign activity in Oregon and California long enough to do some arithmetic. And just as suddenly the public was confronted with such headlines as "Can Barry Goldwater Be Stopped?" *Newsweek* received reports from political writers in each of the 50 states and concluded with some surprise that Goldwater probably would have in the neighborhood of 600 votes on the first ballot at the convention (655 would be required for the nomination). The same issue of *Newsweek* reported the latest findings of the Louis Harris poll: barely 15 per cent of the Republicans in the country picked Barry Goldwater as their first choice for President. It was almost inconceivable that a candidate who did so poorly in the polls of rank-and-file Republicans, whose personal campaigning had been so unimpressive, would have nearly half of the convention delegates on his side. It was almost inconceivable, anyway, until you considered the zeal of his workers, the careful attention of his managers to the long grind of getting Goldwater people into positions of power at the local level, the absolute dedication of the militant conservative community since late 1960 to achieving the magic number of 655 convention votes for Barry Goldwater. To accept the proposition that Goldwater was on the brink of the nomination, you also had to consider the dreamy disarray of the Republican moderates—the farcical performance, or non-performance, of the fabled Eastern Establishment, which was turning out to be the least awesome bogeyman ever to come down the road.

---

to more than 3,400 Republican county chairmen, and half replied. Student delegation chairmen corresponded with party leaders throughout the country, met with many for interviews, even sought advice by long-distance telephone during the balloting in a serious effort to rise above collegiate whim, or sink below it, and accurately reflect the opinions of the delegates who would vote at San Francisco.

The big movers and shakers who had beaten Taft with Eisenhower did not have another Eisenhower, and they were not sure what to do. The old Eisenhower was receiving earnest Republican worriers at his farm at Gettysburg and at his vacation house at Palm Desert, California, but he was sending them away still earnestly worried. The former President thought Scranton of Pennsylvania might well be the man for the job, but General Eisenhower was not going to drag Scranton out by the ears and he was not going to denounce Goldwater. Scranton, as various journalistic poets were inspired to write, was playing Hamlet at Harrisburg. Lodge remained in South Vietnam, and no amount of fan mail seemed enough to bring him home. Nixon was always on the fringe, lurking, waiting to move in if somebody stopped Goldwater, unwilling to take a hand in stopping him because he would need Goldwater's help to win the nomination for himself if somebody did stop Goldwater. It was the most delicately balanced position of ambiguity in which Nixon had ever found himself—and that was saying a great deal. Everybody was waiting for somebody else to stop Goldwater. And everybody was dreaming about the polls: surely a man without broad popular support could not win. Everybody waited and everybody dreamed but Nelson Rockefeller. He hustled up and down California and Oregon expending energy and money at a fearful rate, trying to get some votes. It was easy to feel a real surge of admiration for Rockefeller; he was doing something. The moderates watched him work and spend his money, and while they waited they speculated on who would snatch the nomination from poor Nelson—you know, the remarriage and the liberal image and all make him unacceptable, poor fellow—if he should manage to cut Goldwater off at the pass.

Goldwater had much to be thankful for. His delegate total was mounting steadily. His opponents were doing more to stop one another than to stop him. His cause probably was strengthened when the backlashers or somebody gave George Wallace 30 per cent of the vote against Governor Matthew Welsh in the Indiana Democratic primary on May 5. The blacklash theory was expected to receive another boost in Maryland on May 19 (and it did when Wallace polled 43 per cent of the vote against Senator Daniel Brewster, another stand-in for President Johnson). Goldwater was not behaving like a winner, however. Three weeks before primary day in Oregon, he canceled all his engagements in the state and virtually closed down his campaign there. He reduced his speaking schedule in California. He quit holding press conferences on any regular basis, and he began to rely increasingly on prepared speeches, de-emphasizing the off-the-cuff talks in which his famous frankness had asserted itself with such unpredictable effects. Goldwater was tired of the campaign trail and weary in his soul of some of the superconservative fans of his that he met along the way.

"You don't know the stuff I have to put up with," he told a reporter, who did know and who somehow liked Goldwater more for being weary.

The general reduction of activity by the candidate reflected more than weariness, of course. It reflected the confidence of his managers and himself. Now was a time for caution. They had the nomination almost within their grasp, and they expected to have a firm grip on it shortly if they did not stumble or suffer some horrendous stroke of bad luck. They were prepared to take a beating in Oregon, probably at the hands of the phantom Lodge, and, although they thought they would win in California, the Goldwater people even believed they might well survive a close loss there.

Nelson Rockefeller won the Oregon primary on May 15 in the biggest upset since Lodge defeated him and Goldwater in New Hampshire. Lodge was supposed to win this one, but distance had pushed the heart too far and fondness had cooled. Rockefeller received 33 per cent of the vote, Lodge 27 per cent, Goldwater 18 per cent, Nixon 17 per cent, Mrs. Smith 3 per cent, and Scranton 2 per cent. Although they were all on the ballot and all but Scranton had boosters working in their behalf, only Rockefeller had put on a strong personal campaign in Oregon. His motto in the last days of the campaign, "Vote for Rockefeller—he cared enough to come," may have been the most important factor in his victory.

He picked up just eighteen delegates in Oregon, but he could go on to California as a fighter who had won something. The Republican moderates thought they had a chance now to stop Goldwater in the best Hollywood tradition—in the last reel. The Lodge people threw their support to Rockefeller with the proviso that they could take it back after he stopped Goldwater in the two-man primary on June 2. When Rockefeller flew into Los Angeles International Airport on May 19—a fine, bright day with a softening veil of smog—he was the temporary representative of all other Republican candidates, at home and abroad, declared and undeclared, real and imaginary.

At a crowded press conference in the Aerospace Room of the International Hotel near the airport ("Most Soundproof Hotel in the World—Come In, Be Amazed") Rockefeller faced nine television cameras, Walter Winchell in person with his hat on, and a hundred assorted news people. The Governor of New York was delighted to be a coalition candidate in California, "where the voters will determine for some time to come the future of the Republican Party." The issue was simple: he was in the "mainstream of American thought" and Senator Goldwater was not. Goldwater not only was outside the mainstream of American thought but he had deserted "traditional Republican principles" for backwardness and extremism. Rockefeller was confident that the voters of California would see their duty and rise to it.

The sprightly Winchell enlivened the press conference considerably. He had a card in his hat, and I thought it was a press card displayed in the old-fashioned way, but closer examination proved it to be a card of membership in the Beatles' fan club. Winchell asked several questions during the press conference, but he saved his best one for the hall outside, where he buttonholed Rockefeller and backed him into a corner.

"I have one thing to ask you, Governor," he said in that urgent voice. "When is the baby due?"

Rockefeller, an old friend, seemed to think it was a reasonable question and quoted an obstetrician's opinion that Mrs. Rockefeller's baby would be born early in June. Winchell said he would appreciate the word as soon as the Governor received it, or sooner.

When the candidate and the press got aboard Rockefeller's trusty bus to begin touring, speaking and handshaking, Winchell joined the troop. At San Fernando State College, where the candidate spoke to several thousand students on the sunny, modern campus next to an orange grove, twenty or thirty members of the audience defected from Rockefeller to watch Winchell make a telephone call to New York.

At the end of the speech, I plunged conscientiously into the crowd to find out what the serious-minded students thought of Rockefeller. I began by asking a young lady in orange stretch pants, with matching blouse and hair, whether she was for Rockefeller or for Goldwater. "I'm a Democrat," she said. "But, tell me, is that really Walter Winchell?" She rushed off to get his autograph, letting the mainstream of American thought pass her by.

The mainstream was the symbol and the omnipresent metaphor of Rockefeller's campaign in California. The main thing about the mainstream, he left no doubt, was that Goldwater was not in it. Wherever he spoke, and he spoke tirelessly at stop after stop from breakfast to midnight, he pointed out Lodge, Nixon, Scranton and Romney in the marvelous mainstream. General Eisenhower was almost constantly wholly immersed in the mainstream. After an invigorating day in the beautiful San Fernando Valley, Rockefeller made a speech in which he widened and deepened the mainstream to accommodate such diverse Republicans as Abraham Lincoln, the late Senators Taft and Vandenberg, and the contemporary Senators Kuchel, Dirksen, Saltonstall and Hickenlooper. He even tossed George Washington into the mainstream. Barry Goldwater never got damp.

Rockefeller was fun to campaign with. His energy was endless, and he could hardly have faked his pleasure in shaking hands and patting people on the back. He was almost always in a good humor, and he didn't mind that the reporters liked to yell at Arnold Collett, the transplanted Kentucky hillbilly assigned to drive his chartered bus in California, "Keep it in the mainstream, Arnold." Arnold Collett, a bus driver with a flair, executed remarkable feats of derring-do on the treacherous freeways and the dusty back roads of the vineyard country. One morning, with the candidate reading his paper in the right front seat, Arnold stopped the bus suddenly on a railroad track, ground the gears, and backed away just in time to dodge a descending crossing gate and an oncoming train.

The candidate grinned without looking up from his paper while the press shouted harsh things at Arnold. When there was a pause in the abuse, Arnold said loudly, "I've had the staff of the President of Mexico on this bus in my time, so take it easy, you guys, because none of you don't mean much to me."

Arnold got lost looking for a television studio in Hollywood. Finally he pulled up near a policeman to ask directions, but before Arnold could speak a journalist thrust his thoughtful head out a window and asked, "Can you direct us to the mainstream, sir?" Rockefeller was sport enough to find this sort of thing at least mildly amusing.

The Rockefeller campaign, it seemed to me, was in the best tradition of primary campaigning in Presidential politics—an expedition full of adventure, camaraderie, desperation, gallantry, foolishness, redundancy and splendid new irrelevancies at every turn. There was something zesty and satisfying about riding through the back streets of Hollywood, lost, with the multimillionaire Governor of New York in a wayward bus driven by Arnold Collett on a mission to save the world.

This was the kind of grand enterprise that made its own folklore as it went along. Nick Thimmesch of Time-Life, who had been covering the Rockefeller entourage since New Hampshire and before, had begun to develop a distinctive shorthand for recurring phrases in the Governor's oratory. The Thimmesch shorthand produced "bomfog," one of the best new words added to the American political lexicon since Mencken. Bomfog originally stood for Rockefeller's repeated statement of faith in the "brotherhood of man under the Fatherhood of God." Gradually the meaning of bomfog was expanded to denote the candidate's standard peroration in its entirety, and by May in California bomfog denoted any passage with tendencies toward bombast or foggy generality.

Supplemented by contributions from other reporters, the Thimmesch shorthand of bomfoggery included such words as fisteg, for "fiscal integrity"; goveclop, for "government closest to the people"; respub, for "responsible Republicanism"; epingrad, for "equal participation in the great American dream"; freeture, for "freedom, the wave of the future";

moat, for "mainstream of American thought"; and mort, for "mainstream of Republican thought."

We reporters could have our smug little inside jokes about Rockefeller's speeches, but he was working hard and his campaign seemed to be going well as far as this one state was concerned. With Goldwater absent from California a good part of the time, Rockefeller had the place to himself and he was determined to see everyone in it.

One morning before nine-thirty, the bus delivered Rockefeller to the campus of California Baptist College in Riverside County near Los Angeles. The candidate bounded off the bus into an applauding crowd of students and was immediately set upon by a large round lady leading a small child and a Pekingese dog. All three—lady, child and dog—had on Rockefeller campaign hats. "Aren't you marvelous!" he said. He shook hands with students as he made his way to a platform that had been set up on the lawn in a little grove of palms and pines. "Fellow Baptists," he said in beginning his speech, and then he proceeded to whack Goldwater for softness on Social Security, the United Nations, civil rights and other essentials of the mainstream. The bomfog content was rather high, but Rockefeller also spoke with feeling about the need for rational, responsible opposition to the Johnson administration. He was interrupted several times by applause and once by a helicopter landing in a nearby beanfield to pick up film for *Life* magazine.

There was a question period, and when that was over the candidate was behind schedule, but he also was trapped against the platform by hundreds of students, a good many of whom wanted his autograph. He signed "Rocky" again and again with a felt-tipped pen. He smiled the obligatory smile when, for perhaps the one-thousandth time in the past three months, a humorist thrust a blank check at him for his signature. Several members of his staff began to push him toward the bus, but he stopped to talk with an old man who said, "I shook the hand of your grandfather, old John D. himself, and now it's an honor to shake yours." The candidate was genuinely interested, and they talked for several minutes before the staff conducted him to the bus. He settled in his seat and Arnold gunned the motor, but a wild-eyed woman leaped in the door and grabbed the candidate's arm. He hadn't had a doughnut. The ladies' committee had cooked up a great batch of chocolate-covered doughnuts, and he ought to have a doughnut and thank the nice ladies. The candidate got out of the bus and had a doughnut and thanked the nice ladies and had his picture taken, smiling, with chocolate on his face. This is how primary campaigning is done.

Five hours later, after a speech at San Bernadino Valley College, a television taping in the college studio, a speech to a convocation of civic clubs (strongly pro-Goldwater) at the Orange Show Fairgrounds in Orange County, followed by a rough question-and-answer session at which Rockefeller was at his best, sharp but good-humored, when the questions were hostile, Arnold wheeled the bus into Disneyland. Arnold turned the troop over to the conductor of the monorail train, and soon Rockefeller was trotting down a ramp into Tomorrowland.

He encountered a Mexican family and spoke Spanish. In quick succession he met people from New York, Massachusetts, Missouri, Japan and Italy. Finally he came upon a California man carrying a small boy in a Mouseketeer hat, and both of them committed themselves to Rockefeller over Goldwater. Down Main Street, U.S.A. (a Disney replica, circa 1900), he walked and talked with a cheerful crowd: "What a pleasure! Isn't this exciting? What a spot! Hi, there! Hiya folks!" He was almost hit by a horsecar there on Main

Street, U.S.A., which would have been a terrible way to lose a primary.

The last hope of the Republican moderates, Nelson Rockefeller, had come all the way from New Hampshire to rescue his party from a bad dream, and there he was dodging horsecars in Disneyland. The symbolism was too strong for me, and I took the rest of the afternoon off to lie down.

About ten days before the primary, when the Rockefeller party flew north for a quick swing through the San Francisco area, I stayed behind in Los Angeles to talk with some Goldwater people. From the airport, where he waved good-by to the candidate, Arnold Collett cheerfully ferried me in the Rockefeller campaign bus to the Ambassador Hotel, where two of the ranking men in the Goldwater campaign were holding a press conference in the absence of the Senator, who had not been in California for some days. George Young, an amiable, youthful political-public-relations man with a professionally detached manner, rode along part of the way in the bus. He was a member of the firm of Spencer-Roberts and Associates, a peculiarly Californian outfit that had contracted, in effect, to put on the Rockefeller campaign in the state.

When similar organizations like Whitaker and Baxter were handling the campaigns of men like Earl Warren in the old days, Young said, political public relations in California consisted mostly of "brand-name selling." Now, however, party partisanship required campaign consultants to deal directly in political organization from the precinct level up. Spencer-Roberts, for example, had undertaken to build a Rockefeller organization in California. (Goldwater had the regular Republican organization tied up pretty tight). The consultants lined up committees, handled the advance work for rallies, negotiated with local politicians, prepared huge mailings to all registered Republicans, and participated in decision-making with Rockefeller's managers from the East. Routine public relations and advertising were subcontracted to less cosmic firms. In the hot competition among political consultant firms in the state, Spencer-Roberts had a top record—fourteen wins, two losses. The wins included the election of one United States Senator, Tom Kuchel; four Congressmen; one mayor; three state assemblymen; one state senator; and three Los Angeles city councilmen.

Young thought the firm had perhaps an even chance of racking up another victory with Rockefeller. "The Goldwater people have the ready-made Republican organization and they have all those volunteer workers," he said, "but they have the problem of trying to get along with the kooks and the nuts. As I see it, that is Bill Knowland's job—he is known as the campaign manager but his job is to keep the kooks and the nuts from embarrassing the responsible people who are working for Barry. I wouldn't want the job. In the end, I suppose who wins this primary will come down to who gets the Nixon vote. He still has a following, or enough of a following to decide between Barry and our man."

The Goldwater press conference at the Ambassador Hotel was conducted by Bernard C. Brennan, the director of the state campaign, which was nominally under Knowland's supreme management, and by Richard Kleindienst, the big, bluff Arizonan who was codirector of field operations on the national campaign staff. They had called the press together to assure everyone, first, that Goldwater had not left the state for good, that he would be back to campaign throughout the final week. They also took the opportunity to issue a statement attacking Rockefeller as a man who had developed no significant support, was "heartily disliked" in the South, was unpopular in the Midwest, was unpopular "with the bulk of the Republican members of Congress and could not materially help in the election of Republicans to the House or Senate."

Kleindienst said after the formal press conference that the California contest seemed very close, "a cliff hanger." He obviously did not think the contest nationally was at all close; he seemed to believe Goldwater would win the nomination even if he lost in California. Brennan had a private poll that showed, he said, 38 per cent of the state Republicans for Goldwater, 27 per cent for Rockefeller. Of the rest, 27 per cent preferred Lodge as their first choice and 20 per cent preferred Nixon. Door-to-door checks indicated that Rockefeller would get much of the Lodge vote but by no means all of it. "A lot of people just won't vote for Rockefeller," Brennan said. "Anyway, this election has become a fight for the Nixon vote."

So Brennan agreed with George Young in the Rockefeller camp. But if the Nixon vote went to Goldwater, wouldn't that end Nixon's last wispy chance for the nomination? Yes, Brennan thought it would; but Nixon's followers individually could not bring themselves to vote for Rockefeller, in Brennan's opinion. Beyond the philosophical and personal differences that they might have with Rockefeller, the Nixon people were bound up with the regular Republican organization, and the regular Republican organization had been bound up by Goldwater. To vote for Rockefeller, the Nixon people would need urging by Nixon himself or his spokesman in the state. If one overt move of that kind were made— and Goldwater's overt-move watchers were ever vigilant— Nixon would instantly become the villain of the ages among Goldwater fans. He would not inherit Goldwater's support in a deadlocked convention, and without it he could not win. Nixon stood to lose either way. "The Nixon people have a dilemma," Brennan said, and the look in his eyes was at once very hard and quite satisfied.

The Harris poll came out about this time showing Rockefeller taking a narrow lead over Goldwater in California. Nearly half of the voters, however, had not made up their minds or just didn't give a hoot. Reporters talking to voters, to find out how they really felt, found that many of them really felt an impressive lack of enthusiasm for either candidate. Although I concluded from what I had seen and heard in California that Rockefeller probably would wind up with a narrow edge in the voting, local political writers warned that there was an oriental cast to the logic of California politics and the outward appearance of things could be deceptive. Goldwater's missionary legions would turn out every Goldwater vote on election day, while a number of citizens leaning to Rockefeller, for want of anywhere else to lean, might well just stay home and watch television or wash the car. Maybe so, but when all was said and done, wasn't Goldwater too conservative for California, and weren't all the kooks[2] who were for him a liability? No, it was more complicated than that, a resident political logician told me. From the point of view of many relatively responsible Republicans in the state, Goldwater did not look frighteningly radical when he had the benefit of comparison with the kooks. In the spectrum of California Republicanism, Goldwater was almost a moderate.

[2] A "kook" is an eccentric, a crank, a nut. In California in 1964 the term implied far-right Republicanism, an excess of zeal, a tendency to impulsive behavior, and proud refusal to concede that political practicality had any place in the American way of life. The term was relative and opinions differed as to its proper application; appearance may have had something to do with it. A little old lady in tennis shoes (Attorney General Stanley Mosk's phrase) was generally regarded as a kook in the political arena. Ronald Reagan was not. The term was used freely by the Goldwater staff to describe embarrassing Goldwater fans. I once heard Richard Kleindienst say, when asked if a fiery-eyed woman he had been talking to was a kook: "Is she a kook? She is a kook's kook—a kook other kooks can look up to."

His negativism on civil rights seemed mild indeed to
people who were accustomed to rallies for the impeachment
of Chief Justice Warren. His coolness to the United Nations
was hardly radical in a state where superconservative clubs,
cells and marching societies constantly demanded that all the
foreign Communists nesting in that building on the East
River be chased home and the American delegation to the
U.N. be tried for treason. Goldwater's vague blustering
about nuclear weapons was not shocking to people who regularly heard the argument that the first objective of a truly
patriotic American foreign policy would be to drop an
atomic bomb on the Kremlin.

A few days before the primary, General Eisenhower suddenly undertook to put everything in perspective. He wrote
an 1,100-word statement for the New York *Herald Tribune,*
which promptly made the text available also to the rival
Times—oh, that Eastern liberal press. The Eisenhower manifesto called upon the party to pick a candidate who stood for
"responsible, forward-looking Republicanism." He said Republicans should continue to support the civil rights movement, reject oversimplified approaches and "impulsiveness"
in foreign policy, and give "loyal support" to the United
Nations. Rockefeller was heartened, of course, and hastened
to spread the word throughout California by television and
otherwise that Goldwater did not fit the Eisenhower definition of Republicanism. Goldwater's first reaction was to say
that he did, too, fit. Then he seemed to realize that he was
wounded and said the statement sounded like the work of
"the nebulous, mysterious wing of the party that I've never
been able to figure out who they are."

Whoever they were—and I had seen no evidence in the past
four months that the members of the Eastern Establishment
really knew who they were themselves—those people back
east had swung a hard blow at Goldwater in the last days

before the voting on June 2. He was already behind in the polls. Conceivably, it was not the best idea in the world to hit an underdog like that. Who could tell?

And so, as the sun sinks in the West, we take our leave of exotic California and return to the conspiratorial East, where there are fewer identifiable kooks but no less bomfog.

GENERAL EISENHOWER, who seemed finally to have made a move against Goldwater, for better or worse, went to New York City on June 1 and saw to it that it was for the worse. He was in town for a typically benign purpose: to attend a meeting of People-to-People, Inc., an organization promoting personal understanding in international affairs. The reporters who met him were interested in domestic affairs and asked him about his "anti-Goldwater" statement.

"You people read Goldwater out of the party; I didn't," the General snapped. Anyone who had seen anti-Goldwater implications in the statement, which had made headlines from coast to coast because it so obviously contained anti-Goldwater implications, was guilty of a "complete misinterpretation." So now there were new headlines from coast to coast.

Goldwater won the California primary the next day. It was close. He received 1,089,000 votes to 1,030,000 for Rockefeller, or roughly 51 per cent to 49 per cent. In an election that close any of dozens of factors—the first Eisenhower statement, the second Eisenhower statement, the smog, the traffic on the freeways—might have made the difference. Maybe Walter Winchell was being politically perspicacious when he made such a point of asking Rockefeller in California when the baby was due. Mrs. Margaretta Murphy Rockefeller bore him a baby boy on May 30 and he flew home on the last weekend of the campaign to see his wife and baby, this private event focusing new attention on the divorce and remarriage issue. Goldwater ran particularly well in some of California's Catholic districts.

With the 86 delegates won in California, the Goldwater managers claimed a total of about 500 committed to the Senator from Arizona. This was in keeping with their policy of understating such claims. Several independent surveys indicated that Goldwater already had more than 600 delegates signed and sealed and could count on considerably more than the 655 required for the nomination.

Now began the Panic of the Moderates, and apparently they were too late even in their panic. When it might have been possible to stop Goldwater, the moderates were mostly dormant or waiting on each other to make a play. The time for effective action seemingly having passed, the moderates lunged into a frantic swirl of activity. To spectators without pity in their hearts, it was a comic performance.

Governor Scranton of Pennsylvania, who said immediately after the California primary that he would not try to stop Goldwater and that he did not know of any "extremely basic differences" between himself and the Senator, went to Gettysburg at the end of the first week of June for a talk with General Eisenhower. After talking for an hour and thirty-five minutes, they issued no statement, but Scranton's staff passed the word to the press that he was ready to fight Goldwater all the way. The staff had the impression that Scranton had the impression that General Eisenhower wanted him to fight.

Republicans of all degrees, and of all shades of hopeful bewilderment, gathered at Cleveland on Sunday, June 7, for the National Governor's Conference. Scranton was to appear on national television that afternoon, and he had a statement in his pocket announcing that he was in the race for President. On the television program, however, he did not take the statement out of his pocket. To the waiting world he looked confused, dismayed and ill at ease, and he did not announce anything except his same old vague "availability," which he defined so haltingly and mysteriously that he embarrassed not only his friends but total strangers.

How could William Warren Scranton, a usually poised, intelligent, graceful man known to be capable of forceful political action, have fallen into this dismal fiasco? Through the Scranton staff, surely the most talkative ever assembled by a governor, the other moderates at Cleveland were informed the next day that General Eisenhower had pulled the rug out from under him. Scranton, who thought the General wanted him to make a fight and knew he needed the General if he was to make a good one, had received a call from Eisenhower just before the broadcast. The General wanted Scranton to know that he would not be a party to ganging up on Goldwater. And what accounted for the apparent change in Mr. Eisenhower's attitude since the conference at Gettysburg? Well, it turned out that Eisenhower had received a telephone call from George M. Humphrey, once his strong-minded Secretary of the Treasury, now a big backer of Goldwater, who warned his old chief not to be a party to ganging up on Goldwater, for fear of splitting the Republicans worse than they were split already. That must have been a staggering prospect, all right.

Nelson Rockefeller, disgusted, said somebody would have to carry the moderate flag but he was finished; he had done all he could. Richard Nixon, who had stood aloof—alertly aloof—from all stop-Goldwater enterprises, said on Tuesday, June 9, that it would be "a tragedy" if the Senator's views were not "challenged and repudiated." He said Governor Romney of Michigan ought to take Goldwater on. No, Romney said, he was merely available. On Wednesday, Goldwater said of Nixon: "I think he has talked his way out of the running. He is sounding more like Harold Stassen every day." On Thursday, General Eisenhower said he was not going to lead a stop-Goldwater movement, but he did disagree with some of Goldwater's opinions. That night, after meeting with a variety of advisers, including Senator Hugh Scott of Pennsylvania and Malcolm Moos, a former speech writer for Mr. Eisenhower, and talking by telephone with moderate leaders around the country, Governor Scranton decided to run for President.

On Friday he charged off to Baltimore to announce his candidacy formally to the Maryland Republican convention. He said Abraham Lincoln would "cry out in pain" if the party abandoned its principles. (Senator Goldwater had cast his vote during this wild and wondrous week against invoking closure to shut off the filibuster that was holding up the civil rights bill.) When he finally came out, Scranton came out full of fighting oratory. "I have come here to offer our party a real choice. I reject the echo we have thus far been handed—the echo of fear and of reaction—the echo from the never-never land that puts our nation on the road backward to a lesser place in the world of free men," he said in Baltimore. By the time he had reached the Connecticut Republican convention in Hartford the next day, Scranton and his speech writers had shaken the tangled metaphors out of their style. "A small but vocal minority has too often made our party sound naïve, irresponsible, reactionary and heartless," he said. To correct that impression and to make clear specifically that Republicans were not opposed to "Social Security, the United Nations, human rights and a sane nuclear policy," Scranton asked the delegates to rally round.

Rockefeller threw his support, as the saying goes, to Scranton and bequeathed to him his big, efficient staff. The Lodge people passed their support along from Rockefeller to Scranton. General Eisenhower said he had long admired Scranton and was glad he was running. Richard Nixon said, "My role will be one of strict neutrality." Playing the role distinctively about twenty-four hours later, Nixon said that Scranton was "not a very strong man," considering the way he had vacillated before his announcement.

Goldwater, whose managers were now claiming enough votes to make a first-ballot victory certain, welcomed Scranton to the race as "one of the outstanding governors in the nation. He will wage a clean, vigorous campaign. He will not duck the issues." Goldwater also said, "The Republican Establishment is desperate to defeat me. They can't stand having someone they can't control . . ." The "Goldwater Freedom Special," a weekly newsletter published by his national campaign headquarters, explained to the faithful what sort of conspiracy they were up against: "Party leaders responsible for the control of Republican nominating conventions for the past 25 years are now lining up behind Governor Scranton. Scranton's own financial and banking ties with this group are traceable to the family fortune. His contacts with eastern publishers are excellent, as well. John Hay Whitney of the New York *Herald Tribune* lent Scranton his executive jet for his first weekend of campaigning. James A. Linen, the publisher of *Time* magazine, is Governor Scranton's brother-in-law."

During the last half of June, Scranton campaigned in Iowa, Kansas, Minnesota, Missouri, Colorado, Kentucky, Massachusetts, the District of Columbia, Delaware, New Jersey, West Virginia, Florida, Ohio and Michigan. Friendly, sign-waving crowds ("Iowa's Rantin' for Governor Scranton") heard him criticize Goldwater for "dime-store feudalism" and "shooting from the hip." They seemed to like this tall, urbane man with his affable manner and quick mind, and they wondered where he had been keeping himself so long. It was a lively tour he put on, but so far as anyone could tell it did not tear loose one vote that had been committed to Barry Goldwater. Scranton kept saying he was interested in principles, not arithmetic, and it was a good thing. Goldwater was still picking up votes from the last of the state conventions, including 58 from Texas, and the Associated Press tabulation showed that he had passed the crucial level of 655 and was moving on past 700.

Still there were people who thought Scranton had a chance. (I doubt that Scranton was one of them; he was campaigning to make a point, perhaps to try to acquire some influence on the kind of platform that would be written at the national convention, but—most important to him personally, I suspect—to erase the memory of that bumbling parody of Hamlet that he had played on television in Cleveland.) The dreamers who held real hope for a Scranton victory concentrated their optimistic speculation on delegates who merely said they favored Goldwater and were not bound to him legally by a primary or the instructions of a state convention. The missed point was that most delegates "favorable" to Goldwater were citizens who had been working for his nomination with almost unprecedented political single-mindedness for two or three years and had been chosen as delegates, indeed, because they were local leaders of his campaign and deserved the honor. The Goldwater power in the Republican Party had been built up months and years ago when Goldwater rooters, through zeal and hard work, had won control of precinct meetings and district committees and had placed their leaders in the positions of power on state committees.

Yet the dreamers among the moderates could look at a man wearing a Goldwater button—a man who read *Conscience of a Conservative* every night before he went to sleep and rushed out to the mailbox in the morning to grab his copy of *The National Review* or *Human Events*—and honestly believe that this man might switch from Goldwater if somebody explained to him that the world was a complicated place and Abraham Lincoln and Bill Scranton knew more about it than Barry Goldwater did.

On Friday, June 19, at seven-forty P.M., after 83 days of debate, the United States Senate passed the civil rights bill by a vote of 73 to 27. Senator Goldwater, who cast one of only six Republican votes against it, said, "I am unalterably opposed to discrimination of any sort and I believe that though the problem is primarily one of the heart, some law can help —but not law that embodies features like these, provisions which fly in the face of the Constitution and which require for their effective execution the creation of a police state." The Republican leader, Everett Dirksen, who had written vital parts of the bill and with Hubert Humphrey had done more than anyone else to shepherd it to passage, ridiculed Goldwater's argument and expressed his pride in the Republican contribution to the historic legislation.

Governor Scranton went to Washington to talk some politics to Dirksen. Looking for a symbol that would encourage a trend away from Goldwater, Scranton suggested that Dirksen make himself available to the big Illinois delegation as a favorite son. Dirksen replied that most of the delegates' loyalty to Goldwater was "as tight as wallpaper," and the old realist was having nothing to do with gallant failures.

The fifty-eight Illinois delegates met in caucus in Chicago at the end of June, and forty-eight of them announced that they were for Goldwater. Everett McKinley Dirksen agreed to make the nominating speech for Goldwater at the San Francisco convention.

And still the moderates found one last hope to rally them: the phantom Henry Cabot Lodge manifested himself in the United States. He flew home from South Vietnam to resign his ambassadorship and join the campaign for Governor Scranton.

San Francisco

THAT uniquely American political institution, the national party nominating convention, consists of a week of preliminaries and a week of business, followed by four years of hangover. The preliminary week of the Republican national convention of 1964 began on July 5 in San Francisco. There was a revolution afoot in the party, but there was something so soothing, cool and breezy about San Francisco that the advance guard of Republicans was unable to disturb the essential tranquillity of the place during the early days of the week.

In Union Square near the monument to Dewey's victory—Commodore George's, over the Spanish fleet at Manila in 1898—the solemn old musicians of the Municipal Band played happy tunes from *My Fair Lady*. Pigeons and ragged philosophers, the regular occupants of the square, were joined by political people who looked slightly chilled in the sixty-degree weather. Some of the supposedly shrewd conspirators from the East had not thought to bring warm clothes to San Francisco in July. Television cameras peered down on the scene from swooping cherry-pickers mounted on trucks parked in the street, but the pigeons and philosophers were not excited. Neither were the political people. Even the Goldwater partisans were strangely at peace.

Across the street, the St. Francis Hotel was draped in bunting and television cables. Inside, the platform committee of the convention was holding its hearings. The moderate members of the committee, the supporters of Governor Scranton, were trying to provoke the pro-Goldwater majority into a fight. But the Goldwater faction was hard to provoke. When the Scranton people suggested that the platform ought to contain an endorsement of the civil rights bill or a condemnation of the John Birch Society, the Goldwater people smiled and shrugged and slipped outside to listen to the Municipal Band. In the end the platform would contain precisely what they wanted it to contain because they had the votes, and they saw no reason to be hard guys during the suggestion period of the platform deliberations.

Several floors removed from the distracting oratory of the hearings, tentative drafts of the platform were being worked over by Karl Hess, the instant philosopher and chief speech writer of the Goldwater campaign, and by Bryce Harlow and Malcolm Moos, both of whom had served General Eisenhower in the White House. There was a suspicion that Hess's words would live longer than his colleagues'.

When the breeze was right, the platform drafters could crack a window and hear the cheerful bells of cable cars climbing up the precipice of Powell Street to Nob Hill. Five steep blocks of Powell Street were the main thoroughfare of the convention city—from the platform committee and the delegates' hotels around Union Square to the lofty command posts of the Goldwater and Scranton campaigns in the Mark Hopkins Hotel at the top of the hill. To get up the hill, everybody—campaign managers and messengers, delegates and reporters—rode the wonderfully rickety, open-sided cable cars. Presumably the candidates would ride in stately limousines, but they were to be pitied for the sport they would miss by not using the most inspired form of transportation in the country, the only roller coaster in the world that is turned loose on city streets, the perfect wedding of poetry and practicality, the swinging, lurching, clanging proof that foolishness can be useful.

Scranton headquarters, which occupied a whole floor at the Mark Hopkins, looked like a typical big-league convention command post, with one exception: nothing much was going on in it. There was an air of waiting for something to happen and of wondering if anything really would.

Goldwater headquarters occupied another floor two stories higher. Both factions had employed uniformed guards to prevent infiltration via the back stairs, and private detectives to counteract any attempts to "bug" the premises with listening devices. Goldwater headquarters, especially, had an embattled atmosphere: visitors' credentials were examined closely, and various sectors including the communications center and the room containing files on the delegates were barred to all but a few staff members wearing the tiny lapel pins that apparently signified the highest security clearance. In the big administrative office of the Goldwater layout, where several women were typing and answering telephones, there was a vast calendar on which were noted scores of pro-Goldwater functions planned for the next ten days. Wednesday night, July 15, was marked "Victory Party."

After leaving the Mark Hopkins at the end of my first scouting trip on Tuesday, July 7, I plunged back down the hill on a cable car toward Union Square. Still a block away, I could see that the three cherry pickers of the television networks had bent down over a crowd gathered at the edge of the square. There was cheering. Drawing closer, I saw the first chanting, sign-carrying demonstration of the convention season. Several pale girls with long straight hair were marching up and down the sidewalk with signs that said "Ringo for President," and the girls were singing, "We love you, Ringo; yes, we do." Ringo, of course, is a Beatle.

On the second floor of the St. Francis, surrounded by the gold decor of the Colonial Room, the platform committee heard testimony from Dick Gregory, the Negro comedian and prominent participant in civil rights demonstrations. Gregory did not employ the hard sell that platform committees are accustomed to. He said the civil rights movement was going forward swiftly, and he seemed to think it would continue no matter what the Republicans decided to say about it in their platform. He did have a question for his white friends to think about: "Who among us is free? I can give my house in Chicago to any white man, but a white man gives his house to me and he is in trouble. Who among us is free? In the days of slavery, we ran from the white man like a slave should. Now we move into a white neighborhood and the white man runs away, like a slave should. Who among us is free?"

The platform committee enjoyed Gregory's testimony, and when he departed, saying, "Thank you very much and God bless you all," he recieved an ovation.[1] Another speaker was the Rev. Martin Luther King, and he was as relaxed and dignified there in front of all those Republican politicians as if he were in some familiar place, such as his own pulpit or

[1] In his monologue at a local night club, Gregory amused politics-minded audiences greatly with this comment, in rather exaggerated dialect, on the articulateness of General Eisenhower's recent statements: "That Mr. Eisenhower . . . he talk like a white Joe Louis."

riding off to jail in some southern paddy wagon. He was the most eloquent speaker of the day, too, and he was applauded vigorously.

Platform committees traditionally demonstrate their deep concern with everyone's problems by listening to almost anybody who asks to be heard; this committee heard Rockefeller, Stassen and spokesmen for the National Council of Churches, the National Education Association, The Rural Electric Cooperative Association, the American Library Association, the AFL-CIO, the Teamsters Union and the Americans for Democratic Action, among many others at its opening sessions. At one point, Senator Peter Dominick of Colorado, a Goldwater man, did turn to a reporter and say, "Next time our party holds platform hearings, I hope we'll invite some Republicans to testify."

Dominick and the rest of the Goldwater majority on the committee were hearing hours of suggestions that were unacceptable to them, but rarely in recent history has a platform committee worked harder to be attentive and polite in its public sessions. Under the chairmanship of Representative Melvin R. Laird of Wisconsin, who was the soul of courtesy and parliamentary fairness, and with the Goldwater managers watching in the wings, the committee was not going to let anyone get the idea that it had a closed mind. For the Goldwater majority, private pep rallies were held at which the themes were patience and restraint.

Senator Hugh Scott of Pennsylvania, who was the Scranton quarterback on the committee, told the press that he was fighting a fog. He said the Goldwater people seemed willing to "accept anything short of the Communist Manifesto" at this stage of the deliberations, but he knew the majority would write the platform it wanted at the end of the week. The Scranton faction's strategy was to make the majority do something ruthless or take some dramatically backward position early in the action, so that public opinion would be stirred up around the country; but the conservatives were not to be tempted, not yet.

In the new Conrad Hilton Hotel, a short walk from the St. Francis, the ballroom ("the biggest in the West") was divided by curtains into scores of cubicles that served as offices for newspapers, wire services and magazines. Down a hall from this press headquarters, whose curtained alleys gave it the appearance of an Arab encampment, there was a big room used for press conferences. Even early in preliminary week, press conferences were going on steadily. The moderates involved in the platform deliberations were especially anxious to meet the press and state their cases. Representative Abner W. Sibal of Connecticut, for example, called a press conference at seven-thirty Tuesday morning (and he drew a respectably large crowd from the Arab encampment). He wanted to condemn the John Birch Society in the platform. You had to get up early in San Francisco to make the afternoon editions back East.

Marvin Kitman, a writer and professional mock candidate for President, arrived from New York and held the customary press conference. When somebody asked him what he thought of President Johnson's war on poverty, Kitman replied firmly, "I don't believe in shooting the poor."

Coca-Cola and Pepsi-Cola began maneuvering in their quadrennial race to see who could give away the most soft drinks in the convention hotels. The struggle had been so bitter at past conventions that fizz-water lines were cut by stealth and public-relations men bellowed angrily at each other in front of the politicians and everybody. This year, as usual, Coke was relying on machines that dispensed the product at the push of a button—no coin required. Pepsi was sticking with its theory that machines might be replacing mankind, but not womenkind, and a corps of beautiful young ladies in snappy blue dresses and bonnets was deployed behind portable counters to hand out the drinks. The girls also were handing out campaign buttons with slogans that changed daily. So far, the most popular button was inscribed, "Pepsi is in the mainstream of Republican drinking."

Emanuel Ress, the political button manufacturer who anticipated the Republicans and Irving Berlin in 1952 by inventing the phrase "I like Ike" for a button, arrived from the East with a selection of new samples. Most of the samples were routine, but Ress was testing things like "What's Wrong With Being Right?" on the Goldwater fans. As he began to feel the mood of the convention, he explained, ideas and slogans would come to him and he would telephone orders to his factory for the speedy manufacture and shipment of timely buttons. Before coming to San Francisco he had gambled on a large order of small buttons bearing the eloquent inscription, "Help," and these were popular from the first. Several moderates wore them to the platform committee meetings.

Henry Cabot Lodge came to town on Tuesday night to take charge of the campaign for Governor Scranton, who would arrive the next day. The reporters who flew in with him landed in the mood of men landing in a war zone. They expected somehow to find a terrible struggle going on in the platform committee and the Scranton faction beginning to move into a more advantageous position, as the Eisenhower forces did in the credentials committee hearings during the preliminaries to the 1952 Republican convention. They had been talking to Lodge, who remembered the struggle against Taft so well, and they had an idea that Scranton also had a chance to overthrow the conservatives. Their mood shifted to realism in most cases when they were briefed on the status of the non-fighting in the platform committee and heard the speculation reconfirmed on the scene that Goldwater had 700 to 750 votes in the bag.

It was a quiet evening. The great mass of delegates would not arrive for several days, and the news-gathering fraternity could sit around in the Arab encampment or in the nearby bars and discuss the fate of the world. Already it was a large fraternity. Hundreds of reporters were on hand, and the three television networks, with their big headquarters suites on the upper floor of the Hilton and dozens of little sub-studios scattered around town, had assigned 1,500 staff members to San Francisco. So the hotels were full of talk, and the crew of NBC's "Today" show was setting up its equipment in the lobby of the Hilton, and in the principal bar of that establishment a thin girl was playing a zither and singing folk songs in a high, thin voice that cut like a knife through the talk of politics. Already the more serious pundits were avoiding that bar.

On the morning of Wednesday, July 8, five days before the formal opening of the convention at the Cow Palace, Senator Carl T. Curtis of Nebraska, who had been designated as floor manager for Goldwater, held a press conference in the Argonaut Room of the St. Francis Hotel. The Goldwater people did not like to ride down the hill on the cable cars and then walk a couple of blocks to the press headquarters at the Hilton or to make the trip by cab or limousine. They stayed close to the St. Francis, close to their communications. The press could come to them. The Scranton crowd went to the press anywhere; they were behind.

The Argonaut Room was ridiculously small and hot. Wedged behind a lectern at one end of it, Senator Curtis blinked in the television lights and squinted through his thick glasses at seven television cameras, their crews, and a horde of reporters, including Walter Winchell with his hat on. He had nothing important to announce, Curtis said, except his confidence that Barry Goldwater, "the nation's favorite campaigner," would be nominated by the delegates "without hesitation." Lisa Howard, the pretty, pushy lady from ABC, signaled to her film and audio men and charmingly interrupted Curtis. What about "the concensus that Goldwater can't win" against Mr. Johnson? Curtis thought he could win. How did he account for the polls that showed Goldwater running so far behind? "Oh, I don't know," Curtis said. When he was pushed on the Goldwater-can't-win theme, he lifted a forefinger and said in a tone of considerable portent, "I'm not from Boston, but in my book it's as bad to split an idea as it is to split an infinitive."

"What was that? What was that?" several people grumbled in the back of the room. And then somebody dropped a film can with a great crash, and Curtis kept talking in the confusion, and we never did find out what he meant about the split infinitive.

Somebody asked him about Goldwater's ambiguity on issues, and he denied that his candidate was ambiguous. Goldwater had been voting in the Senate since 1953 and his record was clear for all to see because "the Senate of the United States operates in a fish net."

"In a fish net?" the man next to me blurted. And somebody in the back yelled, "Ask the questions louder so we can hear." The man on the other side of me said, "Did he say he had an infinitive in a fish net?" He grinned—he had given up and put his notebook in his pocket—and I missed the next question. The one after that was, "Senator Curtis, has there been any erosion of Goldwater's support?" Curtis replied clearly, "It's picking up."

In the corridor outside the Argonaut Room there was an opportunity to talk with F. Clifton White, the codirector of field operations in the Goldwater campaign. A cool, comfortable, soft-spoken man of forty-six, White had traveled around the country for more than two years as director of the "Draft Goldwater" movement, and now he had left his job as a political-public-relations consultant in New York to work full time on the candidate's staff. More than anyone else on the staff, he was responsible for marshaling Goldwater's army of delegates, and San Francisco was full of rumors that he would be chosen as the next chairman of the Republican National Committee. He was flattered by the thought, but there was nothing he could say about it. He could say, and did in a very believable way, that there was no doubt at all in his mind that Goldwater would be nominated easily on the first ballot. White was asked about the other big rumor of the day: that Representative William E. Miller of New York, the contemporary national chairman, was Goldwater's choice for the Vice-Presidential nomination. White smiled and shrugged. The Miller choice was discussed rather openly around Goldwater headquarters during the day, and it came to be accepted as a really Grade A rumor by everyone except a few journalistic eccentrics and a few of the moderate Republicans who thought Goldwater would turn in the end to somebody who would help him to get votes—namely Scranton, if he would accept the assignment.

Scranton himself arrived in San Francisco Wednesday afternoon. He had spent part of the morning in Chicago, where he had said that Goldwater had "clearly disqualified himself" for the nomination by things he had said and that now the Senator was trying to "defoliate the Republican Party." His friend Lodge had spent part of the morning telling the platform committee to renounce a "trigger-happy foreign policy" and Goldwater's backward position on civil rights.

At an airport press conference, Scranton said he was not thinking about what he would say to an invitation to run for

Vice-President because "there is no possiblity of that." He meant to run for President, he said, and he had a "two-to-one lead in every poll around the country." He sensed "tremendous momentum" for his campaign.

Scranton's supporters gathered to meet him on the brick driveway in front of the Mark Hopkins Hotel on Nob Hill. The supporters were mostly youngsters of college and high-school age carrying Scranton signs (which had been lettered on the reverse side of old Rockefeller placards). The breeze was cool and the sunshine was magnificent there on the hill as the crowd of several hundred people waited for the candidate to drive in from the airport. A Chinese drum corps, pretty little girls dressed in pink pajamas, made a great rhythmic thumping, while the cable-car bells rang off beat in the background and from time to time a four-man band played Dixieland. The candidate was late. A young man from his headquarters had to pay the four-man band in cash to keep them playing for another half hour.

The crowd drew more of a crowd, and soon there were more than a thousand of us in front of the hotel. Two cheerleaders appeared from somewhere and put on papier-mâché horses' heads, for some reason, and led a cheer with pompons: "Hey, hey! Ho, ho! Come on, Scranton; let's go!" The television crews were shooting everything in sight, and men would say into microphones occasionally, "We are awaiting the arrival of Governor Scranton . . ."

Now youngsters carrying Goldwater signs began to move in at the rear of the crowd. They were led personally by Kent Courtney, the superconservative from New Orleans whose inspired enthusiasm for Goldwater gave chills to soft-sell men like Clif White. Courtney had distributed a broadside in San Francisco asking volunteers to report to the headquarters of "The Independent Americans for Goldwater" headquarters on Mission Street to do important work for Goldwater.[2] The broadside said, among many things: "We will have on hand 2,000 Goldwater-for-President placards mounted on sticks for the use of paraders and demonstrators. It will be psychologically important for the delegates to see crowds of Goldwater supporters carrying placards in every part of the city. We will assign teams of men and women and boys and girls to constantly carry the placards wherever the TV cameras are set up in order to impress the nation with the overwhelming popular support and demand for Goldwater."

When the Goldwater troop infiltrated the Scranton reception, Courtney himself, a plump, oddly jovial-looking man, was carrying a sign in each hand. One said "Goldwater for President," the other "Stamp Out Scranton." The television cameras moved up close to the action as the Goldwater people tried to hold their signs in front of the Scranton signs. Some mild scuffling ensued, and a good many police moved in. A lad managed to extricate himself from the pack and run up close to the cameras with a sign that said "Go with Goldwater," the words superimposed on a bold drawing of a mushroom cloud.

Then there was a peaceful gesture from Goldwater headquarters itself. Down from a window high in the hotel came a long streamer inscribed "Goldwater says hello, Bill Scranton." The television cameras swung to that, but it blew loose from its moorings and drifted away in the wind. Police sirens heralded the approach of Governor Scranton. The Chinese

[2] The same broadside announced an "Independent Americans for Goldwater Rally" to be held on Saturday, July 11. J. Bracken Lee, Former Governor of Utah, would speak on "How the Nomination was Stolen from Taft in 1952"—a "personal, eye-witness recollection." Tom Anderson of Nashville, Tennessee, publisher of *Farm & Ranch* magazine, also would speak. He was described on the broadside as "a member of the Council of the John Birch Society and . . . America's foremost philosopher-humorist." His speech was entitled "Nominate Goldwater, Or Else."

drum corps set up a tremendous thumping, and the crowd absorbed the candidate's car as the television crews groused and shouted. Scranton got out of the car waving and smiling. His rooters screamed and surged forward, pinning the candidate against the car and threatening to trample him in their enthusiasm. Then, probably by pure luck, the crush of the crowd carried Scranton into the hotel like a chip in a mill race. He was swept along backward, waving a little desperately. As he went up on the elevator to the royal suite, his faction stomped and chanted in the lobby, "Bill will win! Bill will win!" Outside, the Goldwater fans chanted, "We want Barry! We want Barry!"

And that is how, in the American tradition, a candidate for President arrives and takes lodging in a convention city.

The next morning Scranton was up early looking bright-eyed and eager on the "Today" show at seven-thirty. He criticized Goldwater for "impulsive" statements in a recently published interview with *Der Spiegel,* a West German news magazine. At ten-thirty A.M. he appeared before the platform committee and spoke of Goldwater's "foolhardy radicalism" and took the opportunity to remind the committee that Goldwater had once said that any party platform was "a packet of lies and misinformation." He was received politely. Afterward, he went back to his headquarters and made telephone calls to some of the leading delegates who were already in San Francisco, asking them to drop by for talks, and he called some of the less leading ones who were still at home getting ready for the trip. He found time in the middle of the day to climb up on top of a cable car on Nob Hill and make a speech through a bull horn.

The platform committee in the St. Francis at the foot of the hill became embroiled in a long and bewildering debate on the ground rules for debating and voting on the planks of the platform that would soon be coming out of the Gold-water-dominated drafting committee; there would be substitute versions, of course, submitted by the Scranton forces. The Goldwater majority had held a secret skull drill at breakfast in a guarded room of the Sir Francis Drake Hotel. They were not taking any chances; when motions and substitute motions and substitutes for substitutes began coming before the committee, every Goldwater backer was to have his wits about him and not panic. Marie Smith of the Washington *Post* wandered into the meeting—she did not know why the guards admitted her—and heard some of the fascinating discussion. A man suggested that one Goldwater leader on the committee be designated to give signals to the others by scratching his left ear for "no" votes and his right ear for "yes" votes. Some of the fifty or so people present were afraid that they would get mixed up about left ears and right ears in the heat of battle, and it was worked out that the word would be given orally to anyone who seemed confused. The gathering was warned that the moderates would try all kinds of tricks. "We are dealing with desperate people, and we must be prepared for anything," a man said. And another put in, "We must not forget that we are dealing with extremists." Everyone laughed at that, and then the conservatives went forth as one to the platform committee meeting.

Barry Goldwater flew in from Washington at one-fifty P.M. on Thursday. He was tanned and relaxed, confident and happy, not at all the dispirited fellow who had left cold, gray New Hampshire exactly four months earlier as a loser. More than a thousand people, yelling in the sunshine, were at the airport to meet him, and the candidate spoke to them from a sort of pulpit built at the top of an airplane loading ramp. He kept a statement about the Johnson administration's ineptitude in his pocket, choosing to talk instead about his grandfather, Michel (Big Mike) Goldwasser, a Polish immigrant who had found his way to San Francisco 112 years earlier. "As my grandfather came to find freedom," the candidate said, "I promise to confirm and extend freedom over this country and over this world." He also said that "all freedom-loving Americans who love the Constitution will march forward to defeat Lyndon Johnson in November." As for the convention, he took the outcome for granted: "The chances are excellent we will win on the first ballot."

Late in the afternoon, Goldwater held a press conference in a big ornate chamber of the Mark Hopkins known as the Room of the Dons. Asked about his views on the platform, he said, "I would like to see the platform committee left alone." He would not "inflict his desires" on the committee, and if he could not accept the platform he would do the "honest thing": withdraw as a candidate for the nomination. (The problem was not likely to arise. At about this time the pro-Goldwater majority on the committee was rejecting rules changes proposed by the Scranton people. On the key vote of the day, the moderates mustered 16 votes among the 100 members of the committee.) A reporter mentioned that Scranton had demanded that Goldwater submit a full text of his *Der Spiegel* interview to the platform committee, so that the committee and the convention could judge whether or not Goldwater's views were so "impulsive" as to disqualify him for President. Goldwater said Scranton could "buy a copy of the magazine" and submit it himself.

The press conference never again really got off the subject of the *Spiegel* interview as Goldwater was asked to comment on various things he was supposed to have said in it. That interview had become the central issue and basic document of the convention. As the freshest source of material for the moderates' contention that Goldwater was a shooter-from-the-hip, and naïve besides, *Der Spiegel* had begun to dominate press conferences, campaign statements, debates in the platform committee, and woozy arguments in bars—yet apparently there was not one copy of *Der Spiegel* in San Francisco.

Everyone was working from translations, or excerpts from translations, or what somebody heard was in an excerpt from a translation, and confusion was rampant. Reporters, dizzy from encounters with Scranton translators, Goldwater translators and free-lance experts in the *Spiegel*-Goldwater-Scranton dialect, had a refrain they sang as they leafed through different versions:

> Ist das not der *Spiegel*text?
> Ja, das ist der *Spiegel*text!

A dazed local journalist named George Murphy wrote an analysis in this vein: "Herr Scranton ist callen in alles das newspaperwritenmen und getellen them Herr Goldwater ist going to allesgeblowenuppen das whole world." Delegates arriving from the East were bewildered to find their convention city entangled in a controversy in a language nobody seemed to understand. Even the West German correspondents were confused. The interview had been conducted in Washington on June 30 by Hermann Schrieber of *Der Spiegel*. He and Goldwater spoke English. Then the transcript was translated into German in the magazine's offices in Germany; not all of the transcript was published. The first excerpts to appear in American newspapers had been translated back into English by American correspondents abroad. There was said to be an original English transcript in Goldwater's Washington office, but his managers were not eager to release it to feed a controversy about impulsiveness. Goldwater said bluntly that they ought to dig it out and release it; he had not said anything to *Der Spiegel* that he would not stand by. Meanwhile, the Washington *Evening Star* acquired from somewhere what it considered to be a reliable transcript of the interview, and this text was rushed to San Francisco by,

among other agencies, the Democratic National Committee.

It was an interesting interview, all right, and it did provide
one of the best distillations extant of the way Barry Goldwater thought and talked about politics and world affairs.
Some uncontested excerpts follow:

Q—Would you go along with the theory that you are an impulsive man and shoot from the hip occasionally, even on important matters?

A—Well, that may be so. But every time I've shot from the
hip, it has later come to be the accepted position of this country.
I remember when they built the wall in Berlin and I was there;
and I said: "Tear it down!" Oh, the American press stood
aghast: "How could this man do this?" Yet it wasn't two weeks
later our ambassador said the same thing, and today everybody
agrees it should come down. Well, I was one of the first to come
out strongly for NATO and for having the NATO forces sup-
plied with our modern weapons.

And everybody says "this man wants nuclear war." Yet today
they are advocating similar policies.

Now, I'll have to admit that I possibly do shoot from the hip.
I'll have to admit also that while I'm not the most intelligent
man in the world, and a lot of people think I'm quite ignorant,
that I've traveled more in this world, I've done more things, I've
experienced more things probably than most men of this Congress. So, I've been exposed to problems and I don't have to stop
and think in detail about them.

Q—But you would go to the brink of war?

A—Yes. Just as your country has used brinksmanship down
through the years and done so very, very successfully. We've
tried, we've been successful and we've gone closer to peace in the
Straits of Formosa, in Lebanon, in Egypt, in Greece, in Berlin
than we have ever been since.

Q—Do you believe that the United States is really strong enough militarily to put Khrushchev's back to the wall like that? Doesn't America rather lag behind in military development and military power?

A—You ask me that question at this moment and I would say that the United States is strong enough militarily to do pretty much what she wants to do with Russia. But if you ask that question again in 1970, I would have to agree that our failure to provide new strategic weapons, particularly in manned aircraft and in improved missiles, will put us behind the Russians. At that point we can expect trouble.

Q—Do you want to give more military strength to Germany, too?

A—Yes. In fact, I'll say this—not because you're here in the interest of a German magazine—that I think the peace of the world depends on a large measure to a constant alliance between our country and Germany.

I think we have to work—although I can't suggest a route—to a united Germany. This is the one deterrent that has always worked against Russia.

An alliance with Germany is, I think, imperative. I think two wars have demonstrated it. And I say this with all due respect to our military: had not Germany in both wars been subjected to the supreme command of men—or a man in any case—who didn't understand war, I think Germany would have won both of them.

Q—What would you do about Southeast Asia?

A—I would make it abundantly clear—and I think President Johnson is tending in that direction—that we aren't going to pull out of Southeast Asia, but that we are going to win, in fact.

Now the next decision becomes based on military decisions. I don't think that's up to a Presidential candidate, or even the President. I would turn to my Joint Chiefs of Staff and say: "Fellows, we made a decision to win; now it's your problem."

Q—What about foreign economic aid? The polls again show that 58 per cent are against, only 30 per cent for it, without too many qualifications. You on the other hand want to give it only to friendly, non-Communist nations, don't you?

A—I don't want to give it. Period. I think that in the days of the Marshall Plan there was wisdom in it then—to help build up Europe. Now Europe stands on her own feet. I would ask our allies to participate in a multilateral fund that could be used for loan purposes, or in the case of no possibility to pay it back, then a grant. But this business of the United States just willy-nilly giving billions of dollars away and receiving nothing in return— I can't buy that. We can't afford it.

Nobody can ever prove these polls. I can take polls that will show you 90 per cent of the people are against foreign aid, but I know how to make a poll. If foreign aid could be voted on by the American people they would reject it. Just like the civil rights bill. If they could have locked the doors to the Senate and turned off the lights, you wouldn't have gotten 25 votes.

Q—Governor Scranton in his latest speeches insists that you wouldn't really lead the Republican Party if you're nominated, but rather force a split and set up a party of your own. Would you?

A—No. And I think probably I have made more speeches on that subject than Scranton has had birthdays. I am opposed to a third-party movement. I believe in the two-party system. I have spoken on it time and time again. I don't know, frankly, who is writing Scranton's stuff. It's getting a little bit on the silly side. He's been a member of my Air Force Squadron for years. We know each other intimately. He knows these things aren't true. I see again he's not going to support me if I'm nominated. On again, off again.

Foreign correspondents fail to see this. A conservative never threatens to bolt his party. The only threats we get are from men like Javits, Keating, Kuchel and Rockefeller. These are the liberals in the Republican Party. They say either do it my way or I won't do it your way. It's we conservatives who get out and break our necks working for the party.

Q—Then there is no chance any more for a Goldwater-Scranton ticket?

A—I would say he has completely ruled that out. At one time there was a very strong possibility for it. But when he has turned to attacking personally a man that I always thought he considered a friend—well, the old *Et tu, Brute.* I think probably if I get the nomination I will have to seek elsewhere.

Q—Will you try to gain control of the Republican Party if you're nominated?

A—I have never had any desire to control the party as such. I'd like to participate in its decisions. I'd like to help in the selection of its professional leadership, but as to changing its directions or writing its dictums, no. I have no desire to do that.

Q—Do you think you would stand a chance to win over President Johnson in November?

A—If you ask that question as of now—and I always like to answer political questions as of now—no. I don't think any Republican can—as of now. But I'll say this: that no Republican can do anything against Johnson without the support of the South. And they cannot support Scranton, Rockefeller or Lodge down there. They could support Nixon to some extent. But they could support me much more completely. How much, I don't know. I don't think I'd be rash enough to say I could beat Johnson in the South as of now. But come Election Day, there's going to be another horse race, I believe.

Q—Then doesn't the idea that you might actually become President of the United States frighten you?

A—Look, the idea of becoming a United States Senator scares the hell out of me. Becoming President is even more so.

Q—Then why are you after it?

A—Well, why does any man seek it? I have often asked myself that question. Jefferson called it the "perfect misery." I can look down there at the White House and see what happens to these people. But I don't think Johnson is better equipped than I would be or probably thousands of men in the country. Nor do I think I am the best man in the Republican Party or the best man in the United States. I just happen to be a politician who decided it was time to give the people of the country a chance to express themselves. And if the expression is no—we've given them a chance. Nothing is changed. Nothing is hurt.

By Friday, July 10, the great mass of the convention crowd was beginning to arrive in San Francisco: the foot soldiers among the 1,308 delegates, the alternates, the spouses and children of delegates and alternates, big contributors, little contributors who had saved up for this trip to see the world saved, platoons of college students come to carry signs, winners of Young Republican essay contests, pickpockets, souvenir salesmen, hot-eyed bands of Young Americans for Freedom, pamphleteers, political-science professors, vacationing weekly-newspaper publishers with press passes but no intention of doing any work, public-relations men and hucksters, entertainers, call girls, café society people who wanted to be "amused"—the standard assortment, in other words, of political pilgrims and camp followers who regularly can be expected at these strange events. By the opening of the convention on Monday, there would be about 25,000 of these visitors in town, according to John Laxalt, a 37-year-old lawyer from Lake Tahoe, Nevada, who had been working since January to fit them all into 140 hotels of varying prestige, convenience and reliability of plumbing. He was the executive director of the housing committee.

I found Laxalt with several harried-looking helpers in a suite in the St. Francis Hotel. Looking for his headquarters among the temporary offices of the Republican National Committee, I passed the doorways of special divisions of the committee identified by such neat signs as "Minorities Division," "Southern Division," and "Reception Center for Foreign Guests and Members of the Academic Community." The symbolism was intriguing, and when I found Laxalt I asked him about it; but he did not have time for symbolism. He had not had time, in fact, to find out whether Goldwater or, say, Margaret Chase Smith was in the lead for the nomination. "Now if you want to know how many suites there are in the Fairmont Tower, and who is in them, and who thinks they ought to be in them," Laxalt said, "I could tell you that. There are thirty-five suites in the tower and there are almost exactly one thousand Republicans, all very important people, who think they deserve those suites."

Laxalt sat at a littered desk on which I spotted two kinds of vitamin pills, a bottle of aspirin and a bottle of tranquilizers. He said he took them at random. When anyone as important as a state chairman or national committeeman called to complain about his room, Laxalt took one of each kind of pill. While I was with him, Laxalt received a call from a man who had been kept awake the night before by noise from a nearby night spot, a shrine of a dance called "The Swim." Laxalt suggested that this was noise to be endured for the Republican Party, promised to look into the matter if it got any worse, and took a vitamin pill, straight. He reminisced briefly and dourly about a call from an important television executive who had been seriously disturbed because some of his staff had been assigned to a hotel "with the shadiest sort of clientele"; Laxalt had fought down the temptation to reply that some of the other guests at the hostelry in question had made approximately the same complaint about the television people.

His face brightened suddenly and he said, "When things

go badly, I try to think about Georgia. Georgia is out at the airport in a motel, away from everything, but Georgia is happy." The basic room assignments for state delegations were made by formula. States received points for their past performances in elections, federal and state, and for their contributions to the party coffers. The high-point states (New York, Ohio, Pennsylvania, Iowa and Kansas, for example) won the prestigious, convenient hotels, such as the Mark Hopkins, Fairmont, St. Francis and Sheraton-Palace. Georgia was a low-point state, cursed as it was with Democrats, and Georgia wound up at the airport. But Georgia was happy there, and had called up to say so, and John Laxalt felt better about the whole Republican Party whenever he thought about Georgia. He had a resourceful turn of mind—I had to give him that.

Most of the delegates arriving in town were well-dressed, more or less cheerful, successful-middle-aged-suburban-looking people; probably there were fewer of the hardened political types than had been seen at any national convention for many years. If the newly arrived delegates were already committed to Goldwater, as so many of them seemed to be, they were welcomed and briefed by Goldwater agents when they checked in at their state-headquarters hotels. Then they pinned on their Goldwater badges, sometimes two or three Goldwater badges, and went out to ride the cable cars, sample the prawns at Fisherman's Wharf, shop at Gump's, make contact with the friendly old jade merchant recommended by their Uncle Henry, have a drink at the Top of the Mark, and generally behave like any tourists in San Francisco. The Goldwater delegates were not much inclined to stand in a hotel lobby whooping it up for Goldwater; there were plenty of youngsters to do the whooping, stomping and snake-dancing. Goldwater delegates were encouraged to enjoy themselves circumspectly, keep their wits about them, and follow a few sensible rules for their own good and the good of the common mission, which was to nominate Goldwater when the time came to go to the Cow Palace and do so.

There was discipline in the ranks of the Goldwater people, but they preferred to think of it as *esprit de corps*. For example, the Goldwater people from eleven southern states were mostly enthusiastic about a mimeographed list of suggestions from John Grenier, the southern regional director of the Goldwater campaign. This document, entitled "Suggested Do's and Don'ts for Delegates, Alternates and Guests," read as follows:

GENERAL

1. DO be friendly and courteous to everyone.

2. DO be very thoughtful and careful when talking to anyone representing the press (radio, TV, newspapers, magazines, etc.).

3. DON'T boo anyone or anything.

4. DO wear your badge, your name tag and your Goldwater button at all times.

5. DON'T spread rumors—stamp them out.

6. DO keep your Team Leader informed of your whereabouts.

7. DO stay in touch with your headquarters.

8. DO relay information to your state headquarters—don't assume we already have it.

SPECIFICALLY—Delegates must be:

A. INFORMED

    1. Read the Goldwater Convention Newsletter, your state's newspapers, and the Oakland *Tribune* which is published by Mr. Knowland. These will be available in your state headquarters.

    2. Watch TV. The Goldwater for President Committee will have three five-minute programs each day on Channel 4, KRON-TV (NBC).

    3. Bring a portable radio. The Goldwater for President Committee will have ten five-minute programs each day on Radio KFAX (1100 on the dial). In addition, important

notices will be broadcast on Radio KFRC (940 on the dial) on the hour and half-hour to delegates and convention participants during the entire week. Radio and TV schedules will be available at your headquarters.

B. EFFICIENT
   1. Carry out assignments and *report back* promptly.
   2. *On time* for scheduled caucuses, meetings, appointments, and bus trips to the Cow Palace.

C. MENTALLY ALERT. This convention presents an unrivaled opportunity to make Republicans from other states aware of the youth, vigor, and vitality of Republicans in the South. Also, remember that this convention will be covered in greater depth and detail by the television networks than any convention in history, and by our behavior we have an opportunity to put our best foot forward to the viewers at home.

Besides being expected to live by the rules, some loyal Goldwater delegates were expected to keep an eye on any stray uncommitted people in their delegations. This surveillance made possible a note I was shown in the Goldwater staff's intelligence file on an unpledged southern delegate. It said, with a notation of date and time: "Initiated a telephone call to Scranton, talked 15 minutes." Thanks to the Goldwater man assigned to keep an eye on this delegate, headquarters knew about the telephone call within minutes after it was completed. An elaborate network of private telephones and short-wave radio allowed headquarters to discuss the situation immediately with the Goldwater leader in the man's state delegation. On the advice of the state leader, a couple of "contact men" from headquarters were dispatched to talk with the object of all this concern. They called headquarters after a time with a new status report on the delegate. He said he was "leaning to Scranton" but had not fallen. Such intelligence on the status and activities of key delegates was brought up to the minute every six hours, and the leaders discussed the best ways of trying to bring them into the fold of the truly saved.

For help in making the best approach, the leaders could consult a file on each delegate, which included a personal and political biography, remarks on his personality, his business, his ambitions, and the names of Goldwater people in his home town and state, in the nation at large, who might have influence on him. The files were detailed and practical. John Grenier seemed to enjoy reading this note to me from one such file: "Mad at John Grenier. Suggest somebody else make contacts when necessary."

Grenier's ideas about organization, intelligence and communications had become a model for the entire Goldwater convention apparatus. Although the apparatus had been set up in anticipation of an all-out battle for the nomination, it was now being used principally for "maintenance of commitment," as the Goldwater staff's *Convention Operations Manual* called it. So far, Grenier had not lost one delegate in eleven southern states to the enemy; in fact, he had gained a few, which meant that his states were approaching unanimity on Goldwater. The reports from the Western, New England, Plains States and Great Lakes States directors indicated to Grenier that commitments were being maintained and expanded all across the country and that Goldwater would have at least 200 votes to spare at the Cow Palace.

The candidate himself appeared before the platform committee on Friday on a congenial bill with Admiral Arleigh Burke, Walter Judd and Walter F. Carey, president of the United States Chamber of Commerce. Goldwater spoke on his usual themes, but he spoke forcefully and sometimes emotionally, and even his opponents conceded that it was the best speech he had made in a long time. He was interrupted forty-one times by applause in the course of what turned into a

Goldwater rally. That big Goldwater majority on the committee had held itself in as long as it could.

Scranton held a press conference at the Hilton. He was surprisingly cheerful and insisted that there was real hope that telephone calls, telegrams and letters from Republicans all over the country—grass-roots Republicans who were beginning to realize that Goldwater would never do—would soon begin to make the assembly in San Francisco stop and think. Scranton was not at his best when being hopeful about the outlook, but he was skillful and forceful when explaining all the things he found to be so unfortunate about the Goldwater candidacy. As a campaigner, he was hitting his stride, impressively, somewhere between three months and three years late.

Saturday was a good day to take the fifteen-minute taxicab ride out to suburban Daly City to look over the Cow Palace,[3] home of the Grand National Livestock Show, the San Francisco Seals ice hockey team, the roller derby, and professional wrestling, and soon to be the home of the twenty-eighth Republican national convention. It is a five-acre building of the blimp-hanger school of architecture standing in the middle of sixty acres of parking lots and cattle pens. Near the main entrance, some policemen were rehearsing controlling riots, and television cameramen on cherry pickers were rehearsing covering policemen controlling riots. At the front door of the building, the ushers were rehearsing sending people to various doors on the sides and at the back.

Inside, the place resembled a Hollywood sound stage. It was lavishly equipped to be the scene of stirring events. The television networks had moved in even before the last profes-

[3] When construction was begun in 1935, during the Depression, a newspaper complained that "while people are being evicted from their homes, a palace is being built for cows." And Cow Palace it was.

sional wrestlers moved out on June 27, and they had built a complex of studios that looked like palaces on the moon for the royalty of the electronic age, although it is doubtful that anyone would go to the expense of transporting so much deep-piled, luminous carpet to the moon. The studios were topped by three glass-walled penthouses overlooking the convention floor. The most striking thing about the delegates' seats down on the floor was the number of telephones mounted on panels beside the seats. Any Republican without a private line was going to feel like an outsider. A man named George Anderson, who was in charge of Cow Palace operations for the telephone company, said he had installed private circuits for Goldwater, Scranton and Rockefeller (whose network was thought to have merged with Scranton's) and for the National Committee, the sergeant-at-arms and the sheriff's office. Counting the telephones for the television, radio and newspaper people, more than 2,000 temporary telephones had been installed in the Cow Palace, and the installers were still hard at work. Private detectives, "debuggers," also were at work, checking the lines for taps.

There was typical pre-show activity throughout the arena. Cameramen on stands in front of the platform shouted at men tinkering with lights on precarious perches up near the ceiling. A creepie-peepie man, carrying a portable television camera on his shoulder, a power pack on his back, and looking into his own monitor mounted on his chest, struggled down the center aisle talking earnestly into a gadget that put him in contact with an unseen but omnipotent guide high in the rafters. Several cameramen followed the creepie-peepie man, taking his picture. One had his camera on a long pole that would allow him to photograph the convention from above the battle. Carpenters and painters were touching up the scenery. One carpenter had on a badge that said "Stop Stassen." A platoon of Young Republican guides strolled by, rehearsing the spiel they would use on visitors. Deputies of the San Mateo County sheriff cruised the ramps and corridors in electric golf carts, stopping to check the bright-red hot-line telephones that they would use to summon reinforcements if things got out of hand.

Robert (Shad) Northshield, the general manager of NBC News, brought John Chancellor, Frank McGee, Edwin Newman and Sander Vanocur, his "floor men," out onto the floor to show them the private telephones and more mystical communications gadgets that would put them in touch with Chet and David up above and the waiting world beyond these walls. "I have the feeling," Northshield said, "that this is the lull before the lull. But if it gets deadly, we are prepared to make our own show." Shad Northshield is anything but a pompous fellow, and this strange talk about making his own show demonstrated how deep was the fear in the television community that the Republicans would settle everything in advance and then come out to the Cow Palace to listen to a few dull peacemaking speeches and to play with their telephones.

At the front of the hall I met a calm young man named James Jewell, who was in charge of temporary construction for the convention. He was proud of the platform that jutted out into the arena. This was no stand of raw lumber and cheap bunting like the one Teddy Roosevelt stood upon to bellow at the multitude. This platform was faced with walnut veneer and would look tasteful and substantial and give confidence on television in the living rooms of America.

There was one piece of timber projecting through the rostrum itself, and I asked Jewell what it was. It was a gavel post, a six-by-six of solid Douglas fir reaching down nine feet to the concrete floor of the arena, on which it was firmly set. When the chairman banged his gavel on top of that post, he would get a resonant sound that the delegates literally would feel in their bones. I confessed that I had thought the chairman banged on the rostrum itself or maybe on a little square of marble. "No, the gavel post is standard at these things," Jewell said. "A chairman needs a big, resonant sound with authority in it, and the gavel post gives it to him."

I felt better knowing about the gavel post. A man knows immediately when he has learned something that will stick with him after these transitory affairs are over.

Sunday in San Francisco began quietly with the cool, sunny good nature of the city still dominating the Republicans on the eve of their convention. At midmorning, visitors strolled in Union Square looking at the residents sleeping on the grass and watching four small Chinese children feeding a shifting cloud of pigeons. A cable car gained the top of Nob Hill above the square and plunged down the other side with a merry clanging. For a time the only sound in front of the St. Francis was the slap-slap of the cable in its channel in the street. A television cameraman dozed on his turret-mounted seat. He had a parasol attached to his camera to shade his head, and he was wearing dark glasses against the glare and a heavy leather jacket against the chill wind. As Herb Caen has said, San Francisco is the only city in the world where a man is likely to wake up with pneumonia, sunburn and a hangover.

Strollers fanned out from the big convention hotels to explore the slopes and precipices of a pastel city, freshly washed by fog, glowing in pale sunshine. From block to block and hill to hill the scenery changed with every aperture between buildings—the Pacific, the San Mateo mountains, the Golden Gate, white sailboats in the Bay, and nearly always the backdrop of a fog bank that seemed to separate a dreamy city from the outside world. Up a hill and down a hill, past a traffic sign

that said "Curb Your Wheels," I came to a street named
Lombard that moved in a straight line for a while like an
ordinary street and then went up another hill in a startling
succession of switchback turns through pink and red flowers.
At the top I sat on the grass and read the Sunday *Times,*
which told of harsh, unpleasant doings in San Francisco, and
I didn't believe a word of it.

The *Times* did urge me back toward the convention
hotels, and soon I was standing in a happy, casual crowd on
California street watching the political celebrities come and
go at the Mark Hopkins. It was the kind of crowd in which
strangers felt free to strike up conversations. Theodore H.
White, the knowledgeable and famous stander-in-crowds at
conventions, author of *The Making of the President 1960,*
was there. When somebody asked him how he accounted for
the outwardly placid mood of the Republican convention,
1964, he gave a measure of credit to the city, but he also said,
"It was all settled so long ago."

Somehow Mr. White had invoked political reality. It was
time to go down from the airy hill and find out how the
platform committee was doing with its chores at the St. Francis. Later in the day, the committee delivered itself of an
8,500-word document in the image of Barry Goldwater.
Chairman Laird said the image was more universal than that:
"It is a Republican platform, and I am sure it will be overwhelmingly sustained by the delegates Tuesday. This document truly represents the mainstream of this convention."
Deadpan, Laird had stolen the moderates' mainstream. As a
matter of fact, the first section of the document—the indict-
ment of President Johnson and the Democrats—employed
another of the moderates' favorite words, "extremist." It
called Mr. Johnson one—a "Federal extremist." It also accused the Democrats of showing "weakness before Commu-

nism" and "playing on the just aspirations of the minority groups."

The positive part of the platform, the promises, spoke repeatedly of "victory" over Communism. On most domestic issues the document was so worded that most Republicans probably would have been able to go along with it, albeit gingerly, but the Scranton-Rockefeller-Lodge people naturally had given it the most conservative possible reading, and they interpreted it as truly backward. Their most important amendments, some meant to be provocative, some less belligerently intended, had been voted down by the Goldwater members of the committee in phalanx. They had wanted a denunciation of extremist groups, and they did not get it. They had wanted an endorsement of Presidential control and prudence in the use of nuclear weapons, and they did not get it. More irritating, if not more important, was the way the moderates on the committee had seen the Goldwater majority routinely steam-roller several proposals for modest, almost meaningless little changes in wording.

Most distressing of all to the moderates was the civil rights plank. It was brief. It promised "full implementation and faithful execution of the Civil Rights Act of 1964, and all other civil rights statutes" and "improvements of civil rights statutes adequate to changing needs of our times." From the point of view of some of the conservatives, whose candidate had, after all, voted against the Civil Rights Act of 1964, that was strong language indeed. It was stronger than some of them liked, anyway, and many of these Goldwater people genuinely believed that the moderates were being ungrateful troublemakers by protesting so loudly. The moderates considered the civil rights plank in the context of what it did not say, the specific amendments that had been so massively voted down, and the moderates were genuinely dismayed. They noted, too, that the drafters seemed to have dragged in by the heels a passage putting the Republican Party on record as "opposing federally-sponsored 'inverse discrimination,' whether by the shifting of jobs, or the abandonment of neighborhood schools, for reasons of race." To the moderate faction, that sounded like a gratuitous appeal to backlashers.

The moderates announced that they would fight the platform on the convention floor. During the day Governor Rockefeller, former Ambassador Lodge and Senators Javits and Keating of New York spoke to 40,000 civil rights supporters who marched from the foot of Market street to the City Hall plaza. The political leaders carefully refrained from attacking Senator Goldwater, but the leaders of the principal civil rights organizations in the nation denounced him at length.

General Eisenhower arrived on a special train that had been wandering across the West from Chicago for two days, picking up Republicans. Mr. Eisenhower, who would be a commentator on the convention for ABC-TV, continued to proclaim his neutrality and to say that he was interested in the unity of the party. Scranton and Goldwater headquarters competed to see who could send the most youngsters out to the Richmond Railroad Terminal to greet the General by yelling and waving Scranton or Goldwater signs. The Goldwater and Scranton signs appeared to be about equally numerous in the crowd of a thousand greeters at the terminal. Senator Goldwater's two sons and one of his daughters were there, if that mattered in the competition. In any event, Mr. Eisenhower, who had been hit on the head by a Goldwater placard the day before when the train stopped at Amarillo, Texas, did not linger long with the crowd. He was hustled away to the Presidential suite on the sixth floor of the St. Francis. A public-relations man for Mr. Eisenhower's network had let me inspect the suite earlier, and it looked like a nice place to stay. In the adjoining studio, where he would do his broadcasts, there were nine red telephones on the General's desk, equipping him admirably to join in this gathering's obsession with telephones.

Before Sunday ended, there occurred in San Francisco perhaps the most remarkable episode in the strange, ill-starred odyssey of William W. Scranton, the reluctant candidate for President who fought so hard so late. A messenger from his headquarters in the Mark Hopkins went down to Barry Goldwater's headquarters and delivered a white envelope marked "Personal." It contained a letter. The most experienced and hardened convention-watchers could not remember anything quite like this letter:

July 12, 1964

Honorable Barry M. Goldwater
Mark Hopkins Hotel
San Francisco, California
Dear Senator:

As we move rapidly toward the climax of this convention, the Republican Party faces continuing struggle on two counts.

The first involves, of course, selection of a candidate.

Here the issue is extremely clear. It is simply this: Will the convention choose the candidate overwhelmingly favored by the Republican voters, or will it choose you?

Your organization does not even argue the merits of the question. They admit that you are a minority candidate, but they feel they have bought, beaten and compromised enough delegate support to make the result a foregone conclusion.

With open contempt for the dignity, integrity and common sense of the convention, your managers say in effect that the delegates are little more than a flock of chickens whose necks will be wrung at will.

I have doublechecked the arithmetic of my staff, and I am convinced that a true count at this minute puts your first ballot strength at only some 620 votes.

Our count differs from that of your managers because we have calculated an important element which they are incapable of comprehending. That is the element of respect for the men and women who make up the delegations to this convention.

We are not taking them for granted. We are not insulting their intelligence or their integrity.

We're not counting noses, we're counting hearts.

We're not issuing orders, we're providing a rallying point for responsibility in the Republican Party.

You will be stopped on the first ballot because a sufficient number of your nominal supporters have already indicated to us that they will not vote for you.

They are not breaking commitments to you; you have broken commitments to them.

You have too often casually prescribed nuclear war as a solution to a troubled world.

You have too often allowed the radical extremists to use you.

You have too often stood for irresponsibility in the serious question of racial holocaust.

You have too often read Taft and Eisenhower and Lincoln out of the Republican Party.

And that brings me to the second count on which the Republican Party is fighting for its soul.

In the last few days the ill-advised efforts to make us stand for Goldwaterism instead of Republicanism has set off ripples of public opinion across the nation.

All of us in San Francisco are so close to the hour-by-hour story unfolding here, that there is a danger we may overlook the over-all impression being created in the minds of the American people.

Goldwaterism has come to stand for nuclear irresponsibility.

Goldwaterism has come to stand for keeping the name of Eisenhower out of our platform.

Goldwaterism has come to stand for being afraid to forthrightly condemn right-wing extremists.

Goldwaterism has come to stand for refusing to stand for law and order in maintaining racial peace.

In short, Goldwaterism has come to stand for a whole crazy-quilt collection of absurd and dangerous positions that would be soundly repudiated by the American people in November.

Meanwhile, we have tried as best we can in the rigged situation engineered by your organization to articulate another point of view.

These are not surface differences between you and the vast majority of Republicans. These are soul-deep differences over what the Republican Party stands for.

We cannot lightly ignore the deep convictions of 60 percent of the Republican Party that Goldwaterism is wrong. Circumstances have given me the responsibility of speaking for their position. Inclination has given you the task of defending far different opinions.

Neither of us can ignore our responsibilities.

I feel that I have nothing to fear from the convention or from the millions of Americans watching it because my position is a right one.

Certainly you should not fear a convention you claim to control, and I would hope that we have not reached the point where you fear to face the nation.

Therefore, I am asking that you join me in a request to allow both of us to appear before the convention on Wednesday prior to the nominating speeches.

Each of us would be permitted to speak on the issues.

Then we ought to have the opportunity to question each other.

Frankly, few people expect that you will accept my invitation.

If that is true, the implication will be quite clear: You have taken comfort in the inflated claims of your managers and you no longer have any regard for the opinions of uncommitted delegates or of the American public.

So, it is up to you. You must decide whether the Goldwater philosophy can stand public examination—before the convention and before the nation.

Sincerely yours,
William W. Scranton

Barry Goldwater read the letter. When his rage subsided, there was a discussion among the candidate and his advisers, and their decision was to copy the letter and send it back upstairs to Scranton without comment. Then several thousand copies of the letter were mimeographed, and runners were dispatched to slip the Scranton letter under the hotel-room door of every delegate, alternate and important Republican in San Francisco. Many reporters received copies from Goldwater headquarters before they knew that the letter had been released by Scranton headquarters.

Denison Kitchel, general director of the campaign and Goldwater's closest adviser, issued a brief statement that was clipped to every copy of the letter distributed by the Goldwater runners.

Governor Scranton's letter has been read here with amazement. It has been returned to him.

Perhaps, upon consideration, the Governor will recognize the intemperate nature of his remarks. As it stands, they tragically reflect upon the Republican Party and upon every delegate to the convention.

There is no further comment which we will make personally. We do, however, commend to the Governor's attention the following portions of a letter written by Abraham Lincoln to his friend Horace Greeley:

"Dear Sir:
"I have just read yours of the 19th addressed to myself through the New York *Tribune.*
"If there be in it any statement or assumptions of fact, which I may know to be erroneous, I do not, now and here, controvert them. If there be in it any inferences which I may believe to be falsely drawn, I do not, now and here, argue against them. If there be perceptible in it an impatient and dictatorial tone, I waive it in deference to an old friend, whose heart I have always supposed to be right."

And so ended the last night of the Republican preliminaries, with the moderates practicing extremism and the extremists quoting Lincoln on forgiveness and restraint.

At last, opening day, Monday, July 13. The Scranton letter
was virtually the only topic of conversation in the hotel dining rooms of San Francisco. Goldwater was described in the
morning headlines as "boiling mad," and his supporters were
manifestly so. They were eating their bacon and eggs in little
clouds of steam. The Scranton supporters were mystified:
what was their man trying to do? They could only assume
that he was trying to make the Goldwater people furious. If
so, he had succeeded magnificently.

Some of us in the fraternity of journalists, not a notably
clearheaded group this early in the morning anyway, carried
our coffee from table to table, prospecting for a colleague
who might have a rational explanation for the Scranton letter. Nobody, not even among the deepest-thinking pundits,
had a theory that he could really put his heart into. Goldwater had perhaps 800 delegates firmly committed; surely
Scranton did not think his letter was going to break them
loose. There were rumors, in fact, that some uncommitted
delegates from Oregon, Utah and Colorado, and probably
elsewhere, were going over to Goldwater after reading the
letter. Several Republican professionals, who had been concerned about Goldwater's shooting from the hip, now were
more unsettled by the vision of President Johnson reading
the Scranton letter aloud to fascinated audiences on the campaign trail. (Scranton headquarters' version of how the letter
happened was not generally known for days. Scranton, after a
conference with Lodge and Rockefeller, had decided to challenge Goldwater to a debate in front of the convention. All
precedents were against such a thing, but what did Scranton
have to lose by trying? A trusted Scranton speech writer, a

member of that impassioned Harrisburg staff, was asked to draft a suitably challenging letter to Goldwater. The speech writer drafted the missive in a state of exhaustion and angry frustration after weeks of hectic work for a good man who was not getting anywhere on a mission of duty and honor. The draft was checked with one of Scranton's most trusted political advisers, another of the Harrisburg group in a similar state of mind. The candidate himself was away from the headquarters appearing on television, visiting delegates and making speeches; he never saw the letter. His name was signed to it by a secretary, and it was delivered. That was how it happened. The explanation, when it came out, did not necessarily leave everyone feeling completely relieved.)

One of the most interesting things about the episode had been the opportunity it gave to the Goldwater management to demonstrate restraint and good will toward men. The response to Scranton, the quote from Lincoln, the fast distribution of the exchange to every delegate—all this comprised one of the master strokes of convention tactics in recent times. If the contest had been close, if a Goldwater victory had not been taken for granted, this might have been historic maneuvering.

As the delegates arrived at the Cow Palace in chartered buses, the Goldwater managers played the theme of restraint. From a trailer parked behind the platform, the word went out by telephone and walkie-talkie to the team captains on the floor: Goldwater delegates were to behave in the Goldwater-Lincoln tradition. No booing of Scranton types, no anger, no counterattack upon the *provocateurs*.

The atmosphere of self-restraint was thick enough to cut with a hatchet when National Chairman William E. Miller stepped to the rostrum at ten-thirty A.M.—a half hour late in adherence to the custom of these conclaves—and intoned the famous words: "Will the sergeant-at-arms clear the aisles. Will the delegates kindly take their seats."

What ensued was the unusual spectacle of the delegates kindly taking their seats and the aisles becoming more or less clear. Electronic agents, sprouting antennae and carrying the fearsome-looking weapons of their trade, continued to patrol the aisles, but the scene in general was oddly orderly. During Chairman Miller's opening remarks about unity, sweetness and light in the Grand Old Party, the thirty-button telephone in the Pennsylvania delegation rang plaintively and a bewildered delegate punched buttons until he subdued it. A man in the aisle beside the Oregon sign shouted into his walkie-talkie, then held it to his ear and shook his head. "A voice keeps telling me I have a fare in Daly City," he said to a colleague, and the colleague said the reception was better in Utah or New York on the other side of the arena.

There was much welcoming oratory by a variety of officials, including the Democratic Mayor of San Francisco, John Shelley, who provided a nice nonpartisan touch by making a speech that was just as dull as the Republican speeches. Eventually the program reached a potentially disruptive event—a minor rules change proposed by the Scranton forces and calculated to embarrass the Goldwater forces on civil rights.

The Scranton proposal was that no delegate be seated if his selection had been influenced by considerations of "race, creed or color." There was a case at hand; an elderly Negro man from Tennessee, who had been a delegate to every Republican convention since 1940, contended that he had been excluded this year because of his race. The Goldwater faction, arguing that the place to propose rules changes was in the rules committee and the place to contest seats was in the credentials committee, opposed the change. The debate was mild. A few boos greeted one or two of the moderate speakers, but the boos seemed to come mostly from the galleries;

the Goldwater communicators promptly gave thought to establishing walkie-talkie outposts in the galleries to make sure that the spirit of Lincoln was maintained there at all times.

Although the moderates hoped for a roll call on their proposal—to put delegates on the spot if possible—Chairman Miller ruled that a voice vote would suffice. The voice vote was taken. The rules change was defeated by a clear majority of decibels.

While the oratory rolled on, I edged up to the rear of the platform and asked a member of the national committee staff some questions about Chairman Miller, who was by now taken for granted as Goldwater's choice for Vice-President. Summarizing Miller's talents as a campaigner, the staff man said, "He's a guy who can look into the TV and snarl, and his mind works fast, and he's willing. Also, he's a gut-cutter."

Soon all the orators on the schedule were used up, and Miller recessed the convention until five P.M. Riding back downtown on a bus and reviewing the opening session, I realized that the biggest cheer of the morning was inspired by Senator Curtis of Nebraska, who had gazed benignly upon the assembled delegates and said, "You are the salt of the earth. . . . You are the hope of mankind."

Although the moderates planned to try once more to provoke the Goldwater faction—and the nation—by making a fight on the platform later in the week, they were hardly hopeful about the prospects. Some did cling, however, to the dim, slim hope that General Eisenhower would manage somehow to say something that would magically turn the tide. The General held a well-attended press conference at the Hilton on Monday afternoon, and this is how it went:

General Eisenhower: I was told when I came in that there would be someone to introduce me to this crowd. I told them that it would be very simple. I will tell you: my name is Eisenhower; Dwight D., that is. And although I have no prepared statement of any kind, I have to recall after the experience of about—I think this is the fourth political convention—that the par for the course is about one flap an hour. There seems to be one right now, and I will try to straighten it out.

This morning, Secretary Gates, who used to be my Secretary of Defense, came to me with a proposal about an item that I believe Governor Scranton wanted. He came on Governor Scranton's behalf, a proposal to put a statement in the platform—and this was the statement—to which we agreed, and which I understand Governor Scranton agreed to:

"The Republican Party reaffirms the historical constitutional precept of civil control over the military. The most awesome responsibility faced by the President of the United States is the control over our nuclear arsenal. The authority to use America's nuclear weapons belongs to the President of the United States."

My comment on this was—and this is what caused the flap a little later when I made the same statement over a network—I said that this statement was perfectly all right with me because it reaffirms what the Constitution means and laws say. And that being the case, I thought that if it was thought desirable to reaffirm this kind of truth, it was O.K. by me, and I certainly made no objection.

Now, some interpretation—maybe someone was more interested in interpreting than in reporting, I don't know. But the interpretation was that I had pulled the rug from under—I forget whether it was Senator Scranton or Governor Goldwater. (Laughter. Big grin by Mr. Eisenhower.)

Anyway, there is where it stands, and I can't see any possible misinterpretation of my meaning, either, when I spoke in response to a question over the network.

Now, if that flap is settled . . . I am open to questions.

Q—General, do you think, sir, that the platform should contain a criticism of extremist groups, and specifically the John Birch Society?

A—Well, I don't believe—I think I have made this clear often before bodies of this kind. I do not believe in condemning any group by specific names. I do deplore extremism in all human affairs except in the two fields of morals and exact science. The extremists are always wrong. And when it comes to the extremes that are found at the far ends of the political spectrum, they are always wrong.

Q—Do you think that the John Birch Society is trying to take control of the structure of the Republican Party, as Governor Scranton charges now?

A—Madam, I haven't the slightest knowledge about the John Birch Society. There is a man who I am told and who is reported to be its head. He has made many statements that I think are nothing short of character assassination. He has made them against many people, including me, and I think that is far from being a service to the American people. It is destructive of our kind of life, because in the long run we like to think we are a self-governing people and we use common sense doing it. I am not acquainted whatsoever with any tenet of the John Birch Society except that I hear they are against Communism. That is just hearsay.

Q—Mr. President, have you changed your mind, sir, about remaining neutral among the major candidates for the Republican nomination?

A—I don't know whether you should say I am neutral. I said that fourteen months ago I took the position that I thought that it was necessary in view of the conditions then developing, and to every individual that I spoke who I thought had a chance of becoming a candidate, or a potential candidate, I made one pledge: that if he would get into the list to continue and promote the dialogue, that it would give us a broad spectrum of Republican thinking, I would applaud it, I would welcome him into that group. I would not support anybody but I would be against nobody. . . . After fourteen months of saying this to individuals and publicly I don't see how I can change now.

Q—General Eisenhower, going back to another flap, earlier

today on a television program I understand you voiced some doubt as to whether the civil rights platform as it is now drawn up by the Republican committee is satisfactory, and I understand that Mel Laird went up and talked to you about it. Would you tell us about the conversation, whether you are satisfied?

A—Well, he came to see me and the way he explained it to me it sounded all right, because I did, over this same broadcast that I spoke about a few minutes ago, I said that I would personally have liked to have seen the civil rights plank followed by a commitment on the part of the Republican Party to make this thing a moral issue for the party and for each Republican; indeed, I would like to see each American—. The law has been passed. We expect to see it implemented and enforced, and I think that each of us has a moral duty, an ethical and legal duty, to do his best to see that it is enforced without violence, to do so, so that we can more proudly hold up our head among nations and not look like someone trying to promote an internecine war. Now, when he came in, I told him that I would prefer to see something like this. He said I didn't have time—he did say that they had words to that effect, and all that I had seen was in the newspapers and that had stopped with law enforcement. He said the moral tone was definitely there, and I said in that case I would be very pleased.

Q—General Eisenhower, I am a Frenchman—

Q (an impolite American interrupting)—Do you think it would serve a useful purpose to have a debate before the convention between Senator Goldwater and Governor Scranton?

A (looking for the Frenchman, distractedly)—Do I think that we should make any—

Q—Do you think it would serve a useful purpose for the convention?

A—This, of course, would be a precedent, and I am not against precedents. I am not particularly for them. But, I will tell you this: I think a thing like this can come about only if the two or three people that might be involved—I think there are three people at least who will be nominated, I mean put before the convention—they would have to agree, and I would think that the convention authorities would have to agree. Then, there might be some useful purpose to be served, I don't know . . .

Q—In a couple of interviews in the past I believe you suggested that Senator Goldwater was somewhat impulsive in his comments. Do you feel that way still about him?

A (grinning, shaking his head)—Well, you are quoting me, and so I can't remember whether I said this publicly or not, but I would say—I am sure that will be misinterpreted. (Laughter.)

But what I meant was—I do say this: it is no time for me to be talking about the particular characteristics of either of these two men, or a third man—I am not talking about their characteristics now. It is too close to the decision point.

After the press conference, the press repaired to its Arab encampment to make what it could of the interview, and General Eisenhower repaired to his suite at the St. Francis (where he had a friendly visit during the day with Goldwater and where he presumably saw something of his brother Milton, who was going to put Scranton's name in nomination, and his son John, who was campaigning with Scranton among the delegations). The buses went back to the Cow Palace—through a genuine California traffic jam, which several delegations endured by singing "Hello, Barry!" to the tune of "Hello, Dolly!"—for the evening session of the convention.

It was a purely oratorical occasion, relieved only by a "reading" called "A Call to Greatness" and performed by Lloyd Nolan and Victor Jory. The amount of relief that this provided was one of those relative things. In any event, there were fourteen speakers, including the keynoter, Governor Mark O. Hatfield of Oregon. He made a well-phrased, middle-of-the-road kind of speech that did not offer much raw meat for the Goldwater faction. He was cheered when he took his whacks at Mr. Johnson and the Democrats, but quite a few of the delegates sat on their hands when he said: "Our faith challenges any who would destroy freedom, whether they wrap themselves in a false cloak of patriotism or an equally false cloak of religion. There are bigots in this nation who spew forth the venom of hate. They must be overcome, and this applies to the Ku Klux Klan, the John Birch Society, the Communist party, and the hundreds of others like them." On the other hand, he was not booed at all.

Tuesday, July 14. It was a day when Goldwater spoke to the Oregon caucus at breakfast and received a few delegates in his suite but mostly relaxed and played with his ham radio; Scranton spoke to the caucuses of Maine, Montana, Indiana, Hawaii, West Virginia, Minnesota and others; Joseph Magnin, Saks Fifth Avenue, I. Magnin, City of Paris and others gave Continental breakfasts and fashion shows for the Republican ladies; the Senator Smith for President Committee had a reception; Richard Nixon arrived at the airport and went by helicopter directly to a restaurant on Fisherman's Wharf; Edith Head of Hollywood narrated something called "Glamour on Parade" for the Republican ladies; an influential Texan for Goldwater said, "We are forgiving people—for Vice-President we have decided to compromise with the liberals on Bill Miller"; the young supporters of Scranton scurried around organizing a splendid "sparkler parade" for after dark; and the big herd of buses made its way out to the Cow Palace for the beginning of the convention session at four P.M.

The session had been scheduled for this hour to take advantage of prime television time in the East. At the last minute, however, the convention managers juggled the line-up to make sure that the most interesting part of the program would not occur during prime time anywhere east of Hawaii. Orginally the report of the platform committee was to have been put to the delegates early in the evening, after which General Eisenhower would speak. When the moderates officially signified their intention of making a fight on the platform, Mr. Eisenhower was moved up in the order. After his speech, the entire report of the platform committee would be read in the hope of putting the nation to sleep, and then the moderates could have their fight.

Senator Thruston B. Morton of Kentucky was installed as permanent chairman of the convention. Known as "the all-purpose Republican," he was acceptable to both factions, and he also happened to be a thoroughly competent man at the tricky business of keeping political conventions from degenerating into farce on a grand and chaotic scale, which has always been their natural tendency. The chairman had to work at his job from the first: the aisles were choked with television communicators; reporters; photographers; messengers; Goldwater's and Scranton's submanagers, spotters, wardens and communicators; and more assistant sergeants-at-arms than ever had been assembled in one hall in the western world. Saying that he demanded "some degree of decorum," Morton urged the sergeants-at-arms to clear the aisles, which they could have accomplished to a reasonable degree, but did not, simply by getting out of them.

Mr. Eisenhower arrived on the rostrum, and several hundred young sign-wavers surged through the doors and into the aisles—youth clears its own path—to give him the traditional welcome. It looked like old times with him standing up there grinning and holding both arms over his head, and even the grimmest conservatives joined in the ovation. He made a mild speech, which was mildly received for the most part. The Scranton faction cheered when he called for a moral commitment on civil rights and denounced radicalism, and the Goldwater faction cheered when he said that something had to be done about crime in the streets. Everyone cheered for unity. Then, almost offhandedly, he said it: "Let us particularly scorn the divisive efforts of those outside our family, including sensation-seeking columnists and commentators . . ."

It set them wild. There was a roar, then a standing ovation, then a steady, sustained snarl that grew in intensity. Delegates shook their fists at the press section and at the television "anchor men" in their glass penthouses. These people really were mad at us. The uproar continued unabated for several minutes, and Mr. Eisenhower stood there at the microphones seeming to wonder what he had turned loose. "Do you suppose they are coming in here after us?" the reporter on my right asked. The conservative editor behind me seemed to hope they would, but he may not have considered whether the crowd was in a mood to be selective. I supposed that David Lawrence, William Buckley and maybe Fulton Lewis, Jr., would be recognized and spared, but the rest of the sheep probably would go the way of the goats. "I am going down to the California delegation and give myself up to Bill Knowland," an eastern columnist said. "He believes in trial by jury."

The din finally subsided and General Eisenhower decided, of all things, to finish his sentence: ". . . because, my friends, I assure you that these are people who couldn't care less about the good of our party." He did it. He set them off again. During the second uproar, several of us hit upon a desperate plan for survival. If they rushed us, we would throw them somebody to appease them—somebody from the Chicago *Tribune.*

After the speech by Mr. Eisenhower, bless him, the great stall on the platform began. While the moderates stood in the wings with their amendments, a platoon of readers from the platform committee read the entire 8,500-word document in an attempt to break the spirit of the television audience. The resourceful networks did not co-operate, however; they concentrated on their "floor men," who were struggling around in the aisles, doing sprightly interviews. NBC, for example, was nothing less than fascinating. In his glass penthouse, David Brinkley said, "The reading of the platform is proceeding and is coming now along toward the end. . . . John Chancellor is down on the floor with some further information. John, would you come in now, please?"

The camera picked up Chancellor, who said, "Well, I'd try if I could, David, but I wonder if I may be under arrest. They—ah—they have been trying to clear the aisles here, and it's an understandable problem . . . with all the people on the floor. And, we were waiting to do an interview at the Alaska delegation and two of the sergeants-at-arms came along and said, 'You'll have to clear the aisle.' We said we were working and they said that didn't make any difference to them, so I sat down. [He was sitting on the floor.] Whereupon a policeman, badge number 21, from the Daly City Police . . . came and tried to eject me forcibly, I think, is what they'll say on the blotter. And, according to instructions from our editors, I am not being ejected, but there are two here now and I suppose that they're prepared to carry me. That's the situation. If you'd hold on for a second, I'll ask and see."

Chancellor asked a policeman what was next, and the policeman said, "You'll be removed by force of the sergeant-at-arms." A civilian directing the police identified himself as Gary Kitwell, and Chancellor said, "O.K. I don't want to debate this with you, Mr. Kitwell. Well, let's get on with it. . . . I believe I'm acting under instructions now from the National Broadcasting Company. I'm about to be removed. . . . Go ahead, gentlemen, remove!"

Policeman: "The chairman ordered the aisles cleared of all the press and that we have to do."

Chancellor: "Does this apply to all the aisles?"

Kitwell: "All of the aisles; all these four aisles."

Chancellor: "That's Gary Kitwell speaking, from the—are you a member of the sergeant-at-arms staff, Mr. Kitwell?"

Kitwell: "No, sir. I'm with the arrangements committee."

Chancellor: "You're with the arrangements committee. Mr. Kitwell doesn't have a very nice job, trying to get the reporters out, but according to the instructions from my editors I am standing fast and the next move in this drama is up to the cops . . . and I just believe they have *their* instructions. There's more scuffling in the aisles down here . . . that you can see. . . . There's a fight in the aisle, right at Puerto Rico. . . . and that nice quiet policeman who was standing next to me, badge number 21 is—is that *Life* magazine?—is manhandling a still photographer out of here, pushing him out with all the skill at his command and several hundred pounds, too. It could be a nasty situation, gentlemen. I'm right here, David, if you're looking for me. . . . They're ignoring me and I'm not sure what my instructions . . ."

The scene shifted briefly to Sander Vanocur, who described the confusion in another part of the forest, and then back to Chancellor, who was saying, "Well, there's a policeman here, badge number 38, who's got a hand on my elbow and there is a sheriff policeman coming forward . . . I beg your pardon. . . . Here we go down the middle aisle . . . you'll have to assist me, is that right? Walk? Uh. It's hard to be dignified at a time like this . . . what do you say, I'm in custody . . . I have been promised bail, ladies and gentlemen, by my office. . . . This way, officer? And for those of you who are watching, I want to assure you that NBC is fully staffed with other reporters who are not in custody by the Daly City police and the San Mateo Sheriff's office. I formally say that this is a disgrace, that the press should be allowed to do their work at a convention on television. And, if static begins to interfere with my signal it is because I am being taken down off the arena now, by these policemen, and I'll check in later. This is John Chancellor, somewhere, in custody."

Brinkley: "John, John, call us when you can, and let us hear from you often."

A few minutes later, Brinkley had good news: "The chief sergeant-at-arms of the Republican convention is now escorting John Chancellor back to the floor, and I can hardly wait to see it. It really was pretty silly; you shouldn't hold the Republicans responsible for it. They were told, the sergeant-at-arms and the police were told, to clear the aisles and, if they wanted to clear the aisles, nobody would object, but they haven't, never have, and, I assume, never will. I've never seen a clear aisle at a convention. Don't see any now. I think they are worse than they were before the instructions were given out."

Huntley: "We understand that John Chancellor is back in business. He is ready to broadcast and he is going to interview now the sergeant-at-arms. Come in, John."

Chancellor: "As I was saying, we were escorted off the floor by the policemen . . . whereupon we met Mr. Robert Carter, who is the chief sergeant . . . [turning to Carter] Now, how do I get back to Alaska?"

It was almost midnight in the East when the reading of the platform ended and Congressman Laird moved its adoption. Now it was time for the moderate faction to offer its amendments. The first was a condemnation of extremists, including the John Birch Society by name. As Governor Rockefeller walked to the podium to speak for the amendment, the moderates cheered and waved their signs and it appeared that a demonstration for him was beginning. Quite suddenly the cheering was swallowed in a wave of boos and catcalls. This ugly business continued for a minute or two before Chairman Morton restored order. Then, as Rockefeller began to speak, he was drowned out again by the jeering. They had found one villain now—the eastern liberal, the internationalist, the do-gooder, the rich enemy of true conservatism, the enemy of Barry Goldwater—and they went at him much more viciously than they had gone at the faceless legions of the press. It must have infuriated them more that Rockefeller just stood there smiling while Morton banged his big gavel. Rockefeller had his say in a firm clear voice, but he was interrupted by the hooting and roaring almost every time he paused. "It's a free country, ladies and gentlemen. . . . Some of you don't like to hear it, ladies and gentlemen, but it's the truth," he said, and he was booed, and he smiled.

Most of the booing, it must be said, was not coming from the delegates, who were seated in the front section of the hall. Most of it was coming from the galleries. But the waves of sound were rolling and reverberating through the hall, and you had to be able to see whether a man's mouth was open to know if he was contributing. For a while, many of the Texas delegates definitely were contributing, and so were others scattered through the front seats.

In the Goldwater communications trailer behind the Cow Palace, Clifton White punched the "all call" button that put him on the telephone to his men in about thirty delegations. He urged them to put a stop to the booing at once. These "team captains," or whatever they were called, managed to bring relative order to the floor of the convention. But the Goldwater communications network did not extend into the galleries, and it took a while for White's agents to get up there and begin trying to reason with the raucous crowd. Some of these fervid souls were making such a racket that they had to be reasoned with one by one, by pushing up close to them and bellowing into their ears. Some of the younger patriots simply would not shut up; they continued to boo for the cause of freedom or victory or something until Rockefeller left the podium.

The Scranton faction also presented platform amendments broadening the civil rights section and reaffirming Presidential control of nuclear weapons. Compared to Rockefeller, the other moderate speakers were treated with grudging tolerance, although Senator Javits of New York got a blast of boos when he intimated that the party might nominate somebody who was ambiguous about nuclear-weapons control. The extremism and nuclear-weapons amendments were defeated overwhelmingly by standing votes. Following a debate on civil rights that never did develop any heat, that amendment was defeated, 897 to 409, on a roll call.

Governor Romney of Michigan (who easily dominated the galleries, by the way, with a robust, earnestly cheerful scoutmaster manner) offered very mild amendments on extremism and civil rights. The Goldwater managers could have accepted them without changing their platform significantly, perhaps getting credit for acknowledging the moderates' point of view. At this point, however, they wanted no such credit. All amendments were defeated, the platform was adopted as written, and the crowd filed out of the Cow Palace at twelve-thirty A.M. Pacific time into an eerie glare of floodlights, where civil rights pickets marched, policemen shepherded them, and television cameras hovered over all.

Wednesday, July 15, nomination day at the Cow Palace.

1 P.M.—An hour and a half before the scheduled opening of the session, serious young Republicans scurry in and out of the great quiet hall carrying armloads of signs, stacking them under the chairs, where they will be available—two or three signs per delegate—for the spontaneous demonstrations. A 900-pound baby elephant is reported to be hidden under the bandstand.

1:10—An intense collegian describes in a whisper some of the plans for the Goldwater demonstrations. Although the rules allow only 150 demonstrators to come into the arena for any candidate, the Goldwater youth plan to bring in 300 more by using alternates' badges and tickets smuggled to troops waiting outside. Doorkeepers and sergeants-at-arms, political appointees all, will not be hardheaded about this. One demonstration organizer to another: "Are those sergeants-at-arms on the east door ours or Scranton's?" Incidental intelligence from a Goldwater organizer: "We have decided not to shoot down Scranton's balloons with pellet guns. We are going to concentrate on keeping Barry's demonstration going for an hour. Twelve minutes is the rule, and about forty minutes is the record. We are going for a record."

1:55—As the delegates fill their seats, George Lodge, son of the former Ambassador, tests his Scranton walkie-talkie, gets static, lays it aside and says, "Maybe next time."

2:35—Chairman Morton opens the session, saying he does not intend to stay up as late as he did last night. Delegates cheer, but the demonstrators in the outer corridors laugh. They mean to keep him up all night.

3:12—As the secretary calls the roll of the states to discover who wants to make nominating speeches, Congressman Joel Broyhill replies for Virginia, "Virginia, home of Patrick Henry the extremist, passes." (Laughter and growls.)

3:15—The poignant, pregnant, classic moment arrives when Everett McKinley Dirksen strides forward, wiping his glasses, contemplating the ceiling, to place the name of Barry Goldwater in nomination. The feathery locks tossing lightly above the mighty brow, Dirksen reaches the rostrum and looks out into the roaring mass. He gazes upon this roiling convention with dignified surprise, as if he had encountered it on an evening stroll. He frowns for a moment and then says in the voice of an elderly librarian confronted by noisy children, "May we have quiet, please." There is quiet, and the muted organ tones pour forth over the multitude in praise of the "peddler's grandson."

3:40—Dirksen's eloquence soars so high that when he mentions the name Goldwater at the end of a line, the convention assumes the speech has ended and the spontaneous demonstration gets off to a false start. He quells it with a gesture, saying, "I prefer not to proceed until the overtone has subsided."

3:50—Dirksen finishes his oration, a light workout for him, and there is the bedlam so long awaited. Four bands play at once. Marchers march. Signs bob and sway. Streamers are fired into the air with little popguns. Horns honk endlessly, fed by compressed air in cans. The building writhes. (The police bar the elephant lest it step on toes.) Dirksen walks slowly to the rear of the platform, mopping his brow, and allows himself a cigarette and a wan smile.

4:10—Chairman Morton demands that the sergeants-at-arms clear the floor of demonstrators, but a good many of the sergeants-at-arms are carrying signs in the demonstration.

4:20—Chairman Morton contrives to bring the convention under control, shouting, "He's going to need votes, not all this hollering and screaming, in November." On this philosophical note, the Goldwater demonstration ends after thirty-four minutes.

5:02—After the Goldwater seconding speeches, before opening the floodgates to the oratory for the names still to be presented, Morton tells the convention that 20,000,000 people in the United Kingdom are watching, thanks to a communications satellite. The mind boggles at what the British will surmise about our quaint colonial folkways before this night is over.

5:15—Senator Kenneth Keating of New York nominates Rockefeller. Demonstration. Seconding speeches.

6:30—Milton Eisenhower of Pennsylvania nominates Scranton. Demonstration (with much genuine enthusiasm). Seconding speeches. It goes on and on. The other nominees are Governor Romney, Senator Margaret Chase Smith, Ambassador Lodge, Senator Hiram Fong of Hawaii, Walter H. Judd of Minnesota.

9 P.M.—Governor Scranton and his lively, pretty wife Mary join his staff in a house trailer behind the Cow Palace to wait for the balloting. Here at the bottom of a long, dark ramp, the caterers' entrance to the arena, reporters and television crews gather in the shadows around the trailer.

10:05—A truck pulls up to the trailer. Two members of the staff come out of the trailer and help the truck driver unload several dozen neat white boxes. The television lights are on, and one of the staff men, groggy, rumpled, bleary-eyed, is opening the boxes. They are full of letters. "Look at this mail, look at it!" he shouts hoarsely. "This man is the people's choice; the people are for him. Look!" Scranton may not know about this strange, frantic little exhibition outside his trailer, but even the television crews are embarrassed and turn off their lights.

10:13—On television in the trailer, Governor and Mrs. Scranton see the beginning of the roll call for the first ballot. Alabama: 20 votes for Goldwater.

10:21—Illinois: softly, Everett Dirksen announces 56 votes for Goldwater, 2 for Rockefeller. Goldwater is far, far ahead.

10:32—Pennsylvania: 60 votes for Scranton, 4 for Goldwater. Rhode Island: 11 for Scranton, 3 for Goldwater. Now Goldwater has 647 of the 655 votes needed for the nomination.

10:33—South Carolina: "Mr. Chairman, we are humbly grateful that we can do this for America. South Carolina casts 16 votes for Senator Barry Goldwater." The crashing cheer in the arena drowns the sound of the television in the trailer. Bill and Mary Scranton burst out of the door. He holds her arm, and they begin to run up the ramp into the storm of noise. They duck into another trailer parked near the top of the ramp behind the platform. A man picks up a telephone and says that Governor Scranton is ready to speak to the convention.

10:40—The roll call is complete. Scranton comes up the steps to the platform under the big tally board that shows the totals: Goldwater, 883; Scranton, 214; Rockefeller, 114; Romney, 41; Smith, 27; Judd, 22; Fong, 5; Lodge, 2. Scranton breaks out of his walk and trots to the microphones. "The sense of this great convention is abundantly clear," he says. "So be the will of the convention. . . . To the victor I extend my very warm congratulations." The convention cheers. "I shall work for and fully support the ticket chosen by this convention. Let it be clearly understood that this great Republican Party is our historic house. This is our home. We have no intention of deserting it. We are still Republicans. . . . I move we make the nomination of Senator Goldwater unanimous."

Thursday, July 16. Barry Goldwater had watched his nomination on television. Before he went to bed, long after midnight, he held a televised press conference in his suite. He was calm and matter-of-fact and went out of his way to say he thought the networks had done a particularly good job of covering the convention. Looking forward to the campaign, he said, "I intend to conduct a vigorous campaign against President Johnson. I assure you it will not be a personal attack. It will be a campaign waged on the issues solely. I've been through campaign after campaign, and I've never believed that anybody enhances their beliefs by delving into rumors and gossip about opponents. . . . I've known the fellow a long time and I have nothing personally against him."

The next morning Goldwater confirmed that his choice for the Vice-Presidential nomination was William E. Miller, fifty, a Roman Catholic from upstate New York; a member of the House of Representatives since 1950; Republican national chairman since 1961; a dapper little man who sometimes looked surprisingly like old pictures of Jimmy Walker; personally affable, quick-minded, a good bridge player; publicly a well-informed, poised, rather hard-eyed orator whose slashing style had caused a partisan friend to honor him as "a gut-cutter"; an old-line conservative who, whatever his talents, was not known for projecting warmth, moderation or mellow statesmanship to his audiences. To replace Miller as national chairman, Goldwater chose Dean Burch, thirty-six, a Tucson lawyer who had been unknown in the national party until this year but who was a good friend of Goldwater's and a man he trusted to get things done politically in a no-nonsense, Goldwater way.

The Republicans returned once again to the Cow Palace and nominated Miller without a dissenting vote. Then the time came when the "next President of the United States" was introduced to make his acceptance speech. In the joyful din of conservatism finally come into its own, he strode forward to the rostrum, and balloons rained down from the ceiling, and the band played "The Battle Hymn of the Republic."

The tanned, gray-haired man of fifty-five—his features sharp and youthful in the white light, his eyes somehow soft and innocent behind the heavy, rakish glasses—stood there in front of the political revival meeting smiling and waving, then frowning impatiently when he glanced down at the message he had brought, then swatting playfully at passing balloons. There he was; who exactly was he? Who knew any more?

He had become a sort of contemporary legend—a jumble of facts, fancies, and other people's contradictory impressions. Probably most of them were true. He was a savior, a man to be feared, a rugged individualist of driving zeal, a trivial hobbyist who had got himself hooked on "this President thing," as he had called it. He was impulsive, whimsical, the soul of conviction. He was the realist who specialized in wishful thinking, the modern philosopher who had not read the old ones, the simplifier confronting a maze of complexity and always saying what he was thinking without pretense.

Pilot of the fastest jets. Old-fashioned man. Author of two best-selling books of conservative dogma. Inventor of "antsy pants," underdrawers with red ants printed on them, advertised in *The New Yorker*. Patriot, sloganeer, practical joker. The sunny conservative, voice of the dour and discouraged.

He had belonged to the National Association for the Advancement of Colored People, helped to integrate his community and his department stores, and voted against the civil rights bill. He also voted against the nuclear-test-ban treaty, the United Nations bond act, the tax cut. He was against compromise in big things and small things, and his definition of compromise meant that in twelve years in the Senate he had played an insignificant role in the legislative process; he stated his position simply, usually clearly, often without thought of political consequences; he rarely involved himself in the difficult give-and-take by which laws are written; he rarely involved himself even in his own party's attempts to find a unified position on issues in the Congress.

He was one of the most refreshing, disarming, candid men in public life, and when his candor got him into trouble he felt betrayed by those with whom he had been candid. Then he forgave them and took them flying in his airplane and made them his house guests. When they tried to talk politics, he was bored and showed them his ham radio equipment. Some of the people he talked with, and who wrote about him, were unfair to him, and some took great pains to keep him from being unfair to himself, and he brooded about which were which.

Collector of Indian dolls. Sensitive photographer of Indians and the beautiful, stark Arizona landscape. Proud owner of a photoelectric flagpole that automatically raised and lowered the flag with the rising and setting of the sun. Costumed performer of Hopi and Navajo dances. Rider of the dangerous white water of the Colorado River. A man who refused to raise both hands over his head before a cheering crowd because he hated flamboyant politicians.

He joked about his rigid conservatism, and when his own jokes did not seem strong enough to him he asked Bob Hope's writers to help him make fun of himself. The frenzied fringe of the right wing—the kooks, the racists, the frightened believers in vast conspiracies—appalled him. He thought, however, that most of the wild-eyed radicals were merely naïve people who meant well. Many of them thought the same about him and used him as a rallying point while they waited for a leader with a wilder eye.

He flew from city to city, day after day, making speeches and raising money in vast amounts for any Republican of any shade or stripe. His approach to a complex problem almost always produced a simple answer, and the more he thought about it, the simpler it tended to become for him. He set off explosions of emotional response when he spoke in his flat, unemotional voice. In a world of frustrating, confounding muddles, he spoke quietly in favor of virtue and simplicity, against Communism and confusion.

Born on New Year's Day, 1909, Barry Goldwater was the grandson of the Jewish immigrant from Poland, Big Mike

Goldwasser, who became a western pioneer in the old tradition; the son of Baron Goldwater, the successful Arizona merchant and Democrat. His mother was Josephine Williams, a nurse from Nebraska, a devout Episcopalian and Republican, who went to Arizona when she thought she had an incurable lung ailment. (She was eighty-nine years old when she saw her son nominated for President on television.) Jo Goldwater was a crack shot with a rifle, won the Southwest ladies golf championship several times, took her children on camping trips in the desert, and regularly beat Barry's friends playing poker. Barry was an indifferent student in high school, and after a year his father packed him off to Staunton Military Academy in Virginia. He was graduated forty-sixth in a class of 104, a cadet captain, winner of the award as the "best all-round cadet." He enrolled in the University of Arizona in 1928 but dropped out in 1929 after his father died. It has been said that he quit because he was needed to take over the department store in Phoenix, but Barry Goldwater has said that he quit because he was bored ("the worst mistake I ever made"). He was married in 1934 to pretty Margaret Johnson of Muncie, Indiana, daughter of a founder and vice-president of the Borg-Warner Corp. He was president of the department store by then, impatient with the day-to-day details of administration but a whiz at merchandising. At the beginning of World War II, he insisted that the Air Force accept him despite his age and eyesight handicaps, finally and successfully using the influence of both Arizona senators, Carl Hayden and Ernest McFarland. He ferried bombers and fighters to India, stayed in the reserve after the war, and became a major general. In 1949 he was elected to the nonpartisan Phoenix City Council. After managing the successful gubernatorial campaign of Howard Pyle, a radio announcer, in 1950, Goldwater ran for the Senate in 1952, defeating McFarland in the Eisenhower landslide. From the first he was

a conservative maverick who stood apart from the Eisenhower administration, which he once called "a dime-store
New Deal." His Republican colleagues made him chairman
of their Senatorial Campaign Committee, and his subsequent
speaking tours in behalf of his friends and conservatism were
the beginning of the Goldwater boom for President. Until
1964 his chances for the Presidency were not taken seriously
by professional politicians at the national level, and perhaps
least of all by Barry Goldwater.

Now, in San Francisco in July, he was the nominee speaking to the convention. "The Good Lord raised this mighty
Republic to be a home for the brave and to flourish as the
land of the free—not to stagnate in the swampland of collectivism, not to cringe before the bullying of Communism.
. . . Now, my fellow Americans, the tide has been running
against freedom. Our people have followed false prophets.
We must, and we shall, return to proven ways—not because
they are old, but because they are true."

He did not want to "deal with Communism"; he wanted to
make it "give way." He wanted to build a free society on "the
sanctity of private property." He wanted law and order in the
streets. "We are plodding along at a pace set by centralized
planning, red tape, rules without responsibility and regimen-
tation without recourse. Rather than useful jobs in our country, people have been offered bureaucratic make-work; rather
than moral leadership, they have been given bread and cir-
cuses; they have been given spectacles, and, yes, they've been
given scandals. Those who seek to live your lives for you, to
take your liberty in return for relieving you of yours, those
who elevate the state and downgrade the citizen, must see
ultimately a world in which earthly power can be substituted
for Divine Will."

The conservatives cheered. The moderates clapped and
waited for the conciliatory phrases that always came in an

acceptance speech. But the most conciliatory words in the speech were: "Anyone who joins us in all sincerity we welcome. Those who do not care for our cause we don't expect to enter our ranks."

That may have left something to be desired among Scranton, Rockefeller, Romney and their followers, but their disappointment soon yielded to shock. Seizing on the supersymbolic words, "extremism" and "moderation," Goldwater said, "I would remind you that extremism in the defense of liberty is no vice! And let me remind you also that moderation in the pursuit of justice is no virtue!"[4]

A thunderous roar came back from the Goldwater faction, while the moderates sat in despairing, angry silence. The convention ended on that note—the mighty cry of victory and vindication of the conservatives. As American political conventions go, this had been a fairly unusual one, its leaders having carefully and masterfully used the occasion to demonstrate that the Republican Party was deeply and bitterly divided as it went into the campaign against the Democrats.

[4] The passage was underlined in the text. Ed Nellor, his press secretary, quoted Goldwater as saying of the passage, "I like those lines."

Atlantic City

As August began, the Democrats were preparing to have a convention and the Republicans were trying to get over one. The Republicans were having a harder time of it.

Barry Goldwater's remarks on extremism—which were treated by his foes, and by some of his friends, as a handy summary of the tone and substance of the convention—had become the focus of growing furor. Governor Rockefeller had said the statement was "dangerous, irresponsible and frightening." Senators Javits and Keating of New York and others of the moderate faction had expressed their dismay. General Eisenhower had said that Goldwater's remarks "would seem to say that the end always justifies the means"; he said that "the whole American system refutes that idea and that concept." The Democrats had joined in, too— Governor Brown of California to say that he sensed "the stench of Facism" and President Johnson to tell a meeting of businessmen pointedly that his administration believed in "a partnership of moderation." Goldwater had begun the process of "clarifying" the extremism statement almost as soon as he had made it, trying to reassure General Eisenhower that "when you led those troops across the channel into Normandy, you were being an extremist," and William Miller had said with a poker face that he did not think Goldwater had been referring to "extremism in political activity or in political action." The radical rightists wrote letters and issued statements urging Goldwater to stick by his guns: they liked it the way they heard it the first time.

Governor Wallace of Alabama had withdrawn as a contender for the Presidency after the Republican convention, saying his mission had been "accomplished." This was taken to mean that the Republican Party was now an acceptable haven for segregationists, backlashers, states'-rights Constitutionalists or whatever labels suited his various followers of high and low degree. The prospect of a migration of Wallaceites into the party of Lincoln further dismayed many of the moderate Republicans.

Along with the political maneuvering and confusion, there had been real tragedy late in July when Negroes rioted in Harlem, Brooklyn and Rochester. There was news of white violence against Negroes in the South, and tension was widespread as enforcement of the new civil rights law began.

Politicians and the political press undoubtedly were sensitive to tragic events and the moral implications of the racial situation, but naturally they also interpreted it in political terms. Actually, one term seemed to suffice: "backlash." It came into its own in August in every worthwhile discussion. Anyone who was anyone was saying it. Anyone who could say it with a properly thoughtful frown, as if he knew precisely what he was talking about, was assured a respectful hearing at any cocktail party or water-cooler seminar in the land. It was the password to the inner councils of both Democrats and Republicans. Heavy-thinking tacticians would drop everything to listen to a stranger who offered to tell them something about backlash.

If you walked up behind a politician on the street and said "Backlash!" in a soft voice, he would jump a foot off the ground—and come to earth denying that he had given much thought to it. If he was a Democrat, he was trying not to look panicky in public. If he was a Republican, he was embarrassed or at least did not want to appear too crassly eager. The truth was that all political people were fretting over backlash most of the time. Pollsters were fumbling for it in a thousand bosky dells, trying to get a grip on it to probe it and measure it. Computers were staying up all night over it. Social scientists were stalking it, losing track of it, jumping at their own shadows and yelling, "It went thataway!" Columnists and commentators were in a frenzy of backlash analysis, catching one another's theories like children catching measles.

In all the speculation on the potential size of the backlash vote, the key numbers were 30, 34 and 43—the percentages of the votes received by Wallace in the Democratic primaries in Indiana, Wisconsin and Maryland, respectively. Even if the lowest number were cut in half, that would mean that 15 per cent of northern Democrats might well express their resentment of the civil rights movement by voting Republican. A swing like that in the North, with the South presumably shifting to Goldwater more massively, would represent a political revolution in America, and the leader of the revolution would be Barry Goldwater.

Comparatively little attention was given to "frontlash," but wasn't it likely that a large number of Republicans would be swinging the other way on the civil rights issue? And wasn't the obsession with backlash obscuring much lashing on issues other than civil rights? Pollsters and reporters often received deceptive—or at least strange—answers when they tried to talk to people about backlash. I explored the subject with a suspected backlasher who insisted that he was abandoning his Democratic past to vote for Goldwater out of loyalty to a member of the Air Force Reserve. His vote was going to be canceled by "wifelash." She associated the Air Force Reserve with all-night poker games.

Extremism was discussed as much as or more than backlash (and often, of course, the two topics got tangled up together). Not only was extremism discussed everywhere, but sometimes it seemed that extremists themselves were everywhere. *Pro-Goldwater Extremists* were distinguished by their belief that anyone who was not enthusiastically for Goldwater was a dangerous, unpatriotic, Communist-influenced do-gooder; they went to work for Goldwater as zealously as they were already working to keep impurities out of the water supply and the library and Communist agents out of the P.T.A. *Anti-Goldwater Extremists* believed that anyone who found the least merit in Goldwater or Goldwaterism was a dangerous, authoritarian, nutty reactionary; they ran around warning their friends two or three times a day that the sky was going to fall any minute as a result of the convention in San Francisco. *Emerging Extremists* were fanatics of various kinds who were coming out into the open for the first time, and they turned out to be just as tiresome as when they were still in their secret societies, hoods and caves. There were a good many *Literary-Emphasis Extremists,* who wrote tracts and letters notable for a profusion of capital letters, bold-face type, dismal penmanship and heavy underlining; they were not good spellers and sometimes forgot to sign their names. *Prostrate Extremists* advocated that everyone should stand up and be counted for what he believed in, and they promoted this idea by lying down in traffic. *Split-*

Level Extremists advocated strict and unceasing enforcement of all laws except those they happened to disagree with, which they regarded as unconstitutional. *Anti-Extremist Extremists,* among whom there was a sort of population explosion, became so outraged at the tactics of various other extremists that they wanted to go out and crack a few of their heads to show them the American way.

Amid all the talk about extremism, Barry Goldwater kept trying to unhook himself from his famous contribution to the dialogue: "Extremism in the defense of liberty is no vice." General Eisenhower, among others, wanted to hear more about Goldwater's ideas on extremism and several issues in the platform, and the candidate made a pilgrimage of clarification to Gettysburg early in August. There it was decided to hold a "summit conference" in Hershey, Pennsylvania, to try to put the Republican Party together again.

At Hershey, Goldwater met with Eisenhower, Nixon, Scranton, Rockefeller and a dozen Republican governors besides. At the climax of the summit conference, Goldwater said on August 12: "I seek the support of no extremist—of the left or right. . . . We repudiate character assassins, vigilantes, Communists and any group such as the Ku Klux Klan that seeks to impose its views through terror and violence." He said he would use the "moral influence" of the Presidency in support of civil rights. He spoke kindly of the United Nations and the Social Security system. And he promised to consult Eisenhower and Nixon on the appointment of his Secretaries of State and Defense. General Eisenhower then expressed his "full support for the Republican national ticket." Everyone present said hopeful words about unity, but nobody really seemed to know what to make of it all.

In the radical right wing of the party there were mutterings of discontent and disillusionment. Some of the people who had whooped with satisfaction at the Goldwater acceptance speech in San Francisco now grumbled that their man had sold out to the eastern liberals.

As for the moderates, many like Governor Rockefeller were notably restrained in their endorsements of Goldwater and the new era of unity. Others, like Senators Keating and Javits and Representative Lindsay, withheld their support and were unkind enough to wonder out loud which was the real Goldwater—the one on the summit at Hershey or the one on the rostrum at the Cow Palace? As much as the conservatives resented this kind of troublemaking speculation by the liberals, some of them were wondering the same thing themselves. It was obvious, anyway, that hardly anybody was letting bygones be bygones.

Meanwhile, President Johnson was making the final preparations for the convention that he was going to put on in Atlantic City, beginning August 24. As producer, director, star and promotion man—and his own chief consultant—on this enterprise, Mr. Johnson had a great many details to think about. There was one problem that amounted to more than a detail, and that was the matter of the nominee for Vice-President.

Since the New Hampshire primary, Mr. Johnson had been aware of pressure building up for Attorney General Robert F. Kennedy, brother of the late President and ambitious scion of the "Kennedy Dynasty," as people kept calling it. By tradition, of course, the choice of a Vice-Presidential nominee was the President's, and he felt that his hand was being forced, which would never do. At the end of July he made a wonderfully oblique statement that put an end to the Kennedy boom. He had decided that it would be "inadvisable," he said, to select any member of the Cabinet or anyone who regularly met with the Cabinet. Out went Robert Kennedy, and with him Peace Corps Director Sargent Shriver (a Kennedy brother-in-law), United Nations Ambassador Adlai E. Stevenson, Secretary of State Dean Rusk, and Secretary of Defense Robert S. McNamara.

Private polls and conversations with political people all over the country had convinced the President that Robert Kennedy would hurt the ticket more than he would help it. (According to the polls, *any* candidate for Vice-President would tend to reduce the number of votes that Mr. Johnson would attract on his own.) Kennedy was closely identified in the South with civil rights measures. Many businessmen regarded him as "anti-business." Many Westerners and Midwesterners preferred someone other than a big-city Democrat from the East. Mr. Johnson also had his eye on a lot of voters who simply would prefer someone other than a Kennedy. Practical politics might have helped the Kennedy cause if the Republicans had nominated Rockefeller or Scranton, for example, but against Barry Goldwater the President expected the automatic support of voters whom Robert Kennedy would appeal to. All the polls and conferences and newspaper columns about the "Kennedy situation" did not distract realists from the elemental fact that Robert Kennedy was too young and too eager for power to be a prudent choice for Vice-President. Mr. Johnson honored the memory of John Kennedy and he was willing to acknowledge the considerable talents of his brother, but establishing a Kennedy wing of the Johnson Administration was something else again. Unthinkable is what it was.

When Kennedy received the word from the President (the day before the public announcement), he was disappointed. Some of the more emotional cultists in his following were furious and spoke of the "ingratitude of that big cowboy." There were rumors for a while that Robert Kennedy was interested in being Secretary of State. Then he turned toward New York and the race for Kenneth Keating's seat in the

Senate. (Edward Kennedy already was in the Senate from Massachusetts. Pierre Salinger, who had been President Kennedy's press secretary, was running for a full term in the Senate from California. With Robert Kennedy moving into the race in New York, the country stood to acquire what James Reston called "a sort of Kennedy government-in-exile.")

Through the first three weeks of August, Mr. Johnson persisted in brooding over the choice of a Vice-President. He commissioned polls. He interviewed virtually every leader in the Democratic Party that anyone had ever heard of. He interviewed some who did not know that he had ever heard of them. He discussed the choice with people who came to his office on nonpolitical business, and he called them when they got home to discuss it again. Yet almost everyone assumed somehow that Senator Hubert H. Humphrey of Minnesota, the majority whip in the Senate, would be the man. When Humphrey would bring himself to assume it, too, as he did several times in this long trial, Mr. Johnson was likely to telephone and ask what he thought of somebody else as a possibility. All this was hard on Humphrey, hard on the other men whose names kept coming up one day and disappearing the next, and hard on the pundits who would be admitted to the inner office at the White House to get the word, as they thought, only to be asked what they thought of, say, Senator Edmund Muskie of Maine as a logical man for Vice-President. Whether or not he was actually in doubt, Mr. Johnson had decided to use the mystery about who would be the Vice-Presidential candidate as the main plot-line of the convention he was putting on in Atlantic City.

Traditionally, a national convention is a carnival that invades some relatively solemn and rational city and drives it out of its mind. In Atlantic City, tradition was overturned and the political carnival met its match. This funny, gaudy, quite preposterous old place had been America's biggest carnival for the better part of a century, and decades had passed since anyone had accused it of being solemn or rational. By the end of the third week of August, Atlantic City was in the process of absorbing the Democratic national convention and turning it into just another big side show on the midway known as the Boardwalk.

The plenary sessions of the convention would begin on Monday, August 24, but the platform and credentials committees had come in several days early to conduct preliminary deliberations in Convention Hall, the celebrated home of Miss America. The Beatles were coming in after the Democrats, and then Miss America herself. Up the Boardwalk toward the Steel Pier, where a flagpole sitter was making big news and Mickey Rooney and Milton Berle were advertised on the marquee, the Democrats' closest neighbors were a beachwear shop featuring sweat shirts lettered "Fink University," "Olympic Drinking Team," and "All the Way with LBJ"; a jewelry shop specializing in Venetian crystals; and a store that dispensed salt-water taffy and hot dogs with sauerkraut. You had to go a couple of blocks to get a chocolate-covered banana. If you kept going that way, as tens of thousands of people did every hour, on foot and in the famous rolling chairs of Atlantic City, you passed endless pokerino parlors, pennylands, snacketerias, auction houses, miniature golf courses, carny rides, frozen-custard stands and funny-hat bazaars, and soon you came to a glass tank containing two electric eels named Walter and Josephine. They had enough power to turn on five forty-watt bulbs and regularly did so for a constantly admiring audience. Who among the assembled politicians could do as well?

On the other side of Convention Hall the Democrats' closest neighbors were Junior Bargain City, which displayed a vast stock of both bride dolls and nun dolls; a neon and plastic palace named Mother's Snack Bar; a Bingo parlor; and then the emporium of Professor Mohamed—"private readings." I had a word with the professor. He was an elderly, swarthy and entirely amiable seer, and he was arranging stacks of blue yachting caps, which he sold between interludes of foretelling the future. Declining a yachting cap with thanks, I asked the professor who would be the Democratic nominee for Vice-President. He thought about it and said he would like to have a look at President Johnson's palm before committing himself. Pressed for a tentative opinion, the professor closed his eyes for a moment, nodded slightly as if receiving a very slight message, and said, "I don't think Rockefeller has a chance."

Walking along the Boardwalk, enjoying the sun and the breeze, dodging the rolling chairs, gazing into the placid eyes of bench-sitters facing not the ocean but the gimcrackery, trying to reach some tenuous understanding of Boardwalk culture, I found that the tendency to think about San Francisco was almost overwhelming. Dwelling on the comparison was a bad idea. While San Francisco may be America's most beautiful and sophisticated city and Atlantic City may be the capital of questionable taste, such oversimplifications are unfair to Atlantic City. It is not in competition with San Francisco to touch the poetic soul of man. It does not pretend to be much more than a carnival by the seaside. With all its overdressed waiters in mirrored dining rooms in faded, filigreed hotels, Atlantic City in its most ostentatious moments does not really take itself seriously. Some of the political visitors streaming into town were taking it seriously, however. They grumbled about the garishness of it all. They grumbled about bad food (not yet having learned where to find good food). They griped about too much walking (not yet having learned that the jitney buses of Atlantic City constitute transportation of inspired efficiency). They were unhappy with the crowds, the accommodations, the heat and the hokum, carefully missing the point that the American political convention had in a sense found its natural home. These pretensions in Democrats were a little stuffy. If they could not be happy in raffish environs, at least they could be encouraged by the prospect that anything the convention did against this background would look positively statesmanlike.

As for Atlantic City's view of this new brush with history, the community seemed to accept its first national political conclave as its due at long last. After all, Atlantic City still likes to think of itself as the dowager queen of resorts, playgrounds and convention centers in this country, the grandmother of Miami Beach, even the great-aunt of Disneyland. A town of 60,000 residents, it has days when it is host to more than 200,000 visitors, and it does not fluster at the thought of another bunch of conventioneers with badges on. Although Atlantic City did spend a lot of money to clean up, paint up and fix up for the Democrats and the television audience, its place in history already was secure as the town that invented the boardwalk, lifeguards, rolling chairs, salt-water taffy, picture postcards and bathing-beauty contests and gave them to the world.[1] Now it felt entirely qualified to launch a President.

On the Saturday morning before the convention opened, I walked slowly down the Boardwalk toward Convention Hall,

[1] The game of Monopoly is based on the street names of Atlantic City, and delegates who knew the game tended to jump to conclusions about their lodgings' prestige, or lack of it, according to Monopoly values. Convention housing officials told them, particularly if they had a bad Monopoly address and were dissatisfied with their rooms, that this was not a sound rating system. On the other hand, some of the biggest dealers in the party were lodged in the Claridge Hotel at Park Place and Boardwalk, and any Monopoly player knew you couldn't beat that.

where the credentials and platform committees and the Democratic National Committee would meet during the day. The day was hot and sunny and the wind off the Atlantic was snapping the flags and riffling the artificial flowers on the lampposts. A flight of kites soared above an eddy of small boys on the beach. There was the smell of pizza in the air, which was disconcerting before nine o'clock in the morning, but it was a nice day. Long rows of reclining chairs, erratically punctuated by yellow, green and red umbrellas, stretched across the sand in front of the big, bulbous hotels. Breakfast sounds were coming down from the second-floor, ocean-front dining rooms, and the last bicycles of the day were turning off the Boardwalk into the side streets, as required by the law that allows bicycles on the seven-mile-long Boardwalk only between six and nine A.M., reserving it the rest of the time for walkers and rolling chairs, which create traffic problems enough.

A few rolling chairs were stirring. A blue one, motorized, came past bearing a Democrat reading a newspaper with the headline, "Democrats Face Squabble at Atlantic City," the squabble being about the seating of segregationist, mostly anti-Johnson delegations from Mississippi and Alabama. The driver of the rolling chair, mounted behind the passenger, was listening to rock-and-roll on a transistor radio. Businessmen were removing the shutters on their booths. The big wheel was spinning at Funcade, and a few assorted citizens had gathered to gamble for packages of cigarettes. The operator of a miniature golf course was sweeping his nineteen fairways. Atlantic City always gives you something extra.

In the shiny new wing of the Deauville Hotel, Roger Mudd of CBS came out on his balcony overlooking the swimming pool to blink at the sun. As he stood there, blinking, he was recognized by a flock of teen-age girls, and they yipped and gooed at him until he retreated into his room.

Mudd had been involved in a dramatic television line-up shift that in contemporary public life seemed almost as important to some people as Mr. Johnson's pending choice of a Vice-Presidential candidate. That is, he had been snatched out of the ranks of working reporters and turned into an "anchor man" in the cosmic scheme of network convention coverage. Mudd was teamed with Robert Trout to replace Walter Cronkite in the lofty "anchor booth" after CBS took a beating in the ratings from NBC's Huntley-Brinkley team at the Republican convention. For Mudd, who had been serving in his new capacity for several days during the preliminary platform hearings, this elevation involved a good many changes in a professional way of life. Among the least of them, perhaps, were his installation in a fancy hotel room—with a balcony that he could not use in peace because he had become a celebrity—and a new awareness that the collar of an anchor man's jacket ought not to ride up on his neck. Such are the problems of news gathering in the electronic 1960's.

Mudd, prompted by a director, gave thought to his collar problem and solved it by having a loop sewn to the lining at the back of his coat, and threading his belt through the loop. It held his collar down admirably, and CBS took heart. Robert Northshield, the general manager of NBC News, viewed the CBS belt loop with foreboding, saying it might well amount to unfair competition. In any case, his own men would demand belt loops and belt loops would become an essential status symbol in the industry. Northshield even foresaw the evolution of a new breed of permanently sedentary television newsmen, men who could not risk standing up lest they be jerked off their feet by their own belt loops.

Leaving Mudd fretting over the latest convention schedule changes, fresh from the White House, I pressed on up the Boardwalk toward Convention Hall. In a building near the hall, Young Citizens for Johnson had established a headquarters, and the first dozen or so of the expected 2,000 Y.C.J.'s were beginning to tack up decorative streamers and bunting and to work on a few prototype handmade posters. Handmade posters were all the rage with young people's groups; I had noticed it in San Francisco, too. Their elders had let them know that handmade posters looked more spontaneous and sincere than printed posters. I asked a counselor of the Y.C.J.'s how things were going, and he said all right, except that the colorful motorized rolling chair full of "Johnson Girls" waving "LBJ for the USA" signs had run into a rolling chair containing some tourists who were thinking of suing, and a young volunteer hauling poster-makings in a Hertz truck had run into a police car and there was hell to pay.

In front of Convention Hall, an ABC television camera, mounted on a platform slung from a giant crane, dipped down over a milling crowd, but the cameraman was not shooting. He was clinging to a cable with both hands to keep from falling off his platform in the sky, and he was yelling to some thoughtful-looking men on the ground about the need for stability. A truck drove down Mississippi Avenue to where it dead-ends against the Boardwalk, and some earnest young people, white and Negro, several in faded overalls, began unloading steel filing cabinets at the side door of the great hall. The cabinets contained voter-registration records with which the Mississippi Freedom Democratic Party would try to convince the credentials committee that the Freedom delegation should replace the regular Democratic delegation from Mississippi. Passers-by stopped to watch the unloading while a promoter from the Steel Pier moved through the crowd passing out leaflets advocating that the famous diving horse replace the donkey as the symbol of the Democratic Party. Nearby, several young men passed out leaflets urging the nomination of Mrs. Yetta Bronstein for President. Mrs.

Bronstein's literature included an open letter to Barry Gold-water, in which she said: "Your recent concern for the safety of American women at night is good for lots of votes. I too was once chased many years ago." The several sign-carrying demonstrators for Mrs. Bronstein included a live donkey, and it is hard to say whether her campaign was helped or hurt when the donkey bit a passing citizen.

After ducking into the basement press room of Convention Hall for a cup of coffee, I encountered Emanuel Ress, the Shakespeare of the campaign button. He had come down from New York to push some of his buttons and to seek inspiration for new ones. "I'm just keeping my ear in gear with no strain on the brain," he said. That is the way Manny talks. "I didn't get to be the button king, you know, by sitting home. I got to be king because I got home late one night and my wife crowned me."

By keeping his ear in gear, Manny had come up with such button slogans as "I Like Ike" (in 1947, five years before it swept the country), "We Need Adlai Badly" (1952), "All the Way with LBJ" (1960), "Half the Way with LBJ" (later in 1960, when Mr. Johnson accepted the Vice-Presidential nomination), "Stop Stassen!" (1948, 1952, 1956, 1960, 1964), and "Who But Hubert?" (1960). Ress did not claim to have originated all these slogans, although he had originated many, but he did tend to get them into production on buttons ahead of his competitors. In Atlantic City he was pleased to be finding a good reception for "Who But Hubert?"—of which he had a modest stock left over from Senator Humphrey's try for the Presidential nomination in the 1960 primaries. Ress personally was wearing a button that said, "I'm a Moderate Extremist," which he regarded as a sort of summary of the Republican convention. Another San Francisco inspiration, "What's Wrong Being Right?"—which Manny had thought of as nothing more than a mildly intriguing eye-catcher—was moving nicely all over the country, especially so in Texas, he reported.

Ress can move with tremendous speed in button production when conditions warrant it. He was in the Cow Palace when General Eisenhower set off the uproar by criticizing "sensation-seeking columnists and commentators." Manny telephoned his button works in New York immediately, and within three hours a machine was stamping out neat, official-looking badges inscribed "Sensation-Seeking Press." They were dispatched to San Francisco by airmail special delivery, and soon they were appearing on the lapels not only of light-hearted reporters but also of certain journalistic titans who had long risen above lapel buttons as signs of a trivial mind.

It was a big day for slogans in Atlantic City. While Manny Ress hustled through the convention crowd spreading his rash of little slogans from lapel to lapel, painters swinging from boatswain's chairs high above the Boardwalk were putting the finishing touches on the biggest political slogan you ever saw. On a signboard half the size of a football field atop the Million Dollar Pier, a stern and handsome portrait of Barry Goldwater had been completed, and beside it the slogan said, "In your heart, you know he's right."[2]

By Sunday, August 23, most of the major Democrats in the United States and thousands of the minor ones had assembled in Atlantic City and a serious political theme could be detected in the raucous clatter of convention nonsense blending with Boardwalk nonsense. The serious theme was peace and

[2] The Democrats conceded that the Goldwater sign dominating the Boardwalk was a nice political stroke by the Republican National Committee, but the Democrats did not just stand around admiring the ingenuity of the adversary. Within a few days a postscript appeared in similar lettering on a similar dark-blue background. Directly under "In your heart, you know he's right," the new sign said, "Yes—extreme right."

moderation within a united party; that is what the convention manager in Washington was striving for, anyway, and the chances seemed good that he would be able to bring off a generally harmonious convention. There was no contest for President or Vice-President, of course. Mr. Johnson still was playing Alfred Hitchcock with the Vice-Presidency, and neither Hubert Humphrey nor any of the remote possibilities was indulging in any overt activity that might look like campaigning. The basic draft of the platform had been written in the White House, and the platform committee in Atlantic City was satisfying itself by changing a phrase here and a word there if anybody important really insisted. The changes were cleared with the chief platform writer at the White House. It was a suitably progressive Democratic platform, but there was little in it calculated to provoke anyone. The civil rights section was mildly phrased; now that the civil rights act, proposed and passed in a Democratic administration, was the law of the land, the platform did not have to bulge with promises on the subject. This was important to the harmony theme because it removed, or minimized, the traditional source of irritation for the southern Democrats, who might have felt their ancient urge to make a scene if the platform's civil rights language had struck them as too strong.

There was one touchy little problem that had the potential to become a touchy big problem. The Alabama and Mississippi delegations were, to put it bluntly as everyone tried not to, full of Goldwaterites. Whatever was done about Alabama and Mississippi, Mr. Johnson did not want a big brawl on television. Nor did he want to give any of the other southern delegations an opportunity to get their sectional backs up and bolt the convention. The polls in Mr. Johnson's pocket showed that he could write off Alabama and Mississippi, but he was determined not to give Goldwater any more breaks than necessary in the rest of the South.

The Alabama and Mississippi delegations were challenged before the credentials committee, which undertook to find the gentlest possible solution that the convention would stand for. As for Alabama, most of the thirty-six-vote delegation was loyal to Governor George C. Wallace and inclined to vote for Goldwater. The Alabama legislature had even passed a law that would keep the national Democratic ticket off the ballot in November. It was obvious from the first that the Alabama delegates would be asked to sign an oath of loyalty to the party and its nominees if they were to be seated in the convention. Most of them, led by the notorious statesman, Eugene (Bull) Connor, former police commissioner of Birmingham, were defiant about signing oaths, but there was not a dangerous amount of sympathy for Bull Connor and friends among the other southern delegations.

Mississippi was more complicated. The regular delegation was challenged by a delegation representing the predominantly Negro Mississippi Freedom Democratic Party, supported by the Congress of Racial Equality and the Student Nonviolent Co-ordinating Committee. This group had come to Atlantic City imbued with the moral fervor of the civil rights movement in a state where people were dying for a cause. The Freedom Party, contending that Negroes were systematically excluded from the Democratic Party in Mississippi, demanded that its delegation be seated in place of the lily-white regulars. Some liberal Democrats throughout the country had been working to line up support for the Freedom delegation, and feeling was running rather high. The trouble was that the Freedom delegation was not legally entitled to the Mississippi seats. To seat the Freedom delegation illegally would cause a terrible furor; to brush aside the moral case posed by the civil rights movement in Mississippi was out of the question.

The Atlantic City branch of the White House—a shiny motel called the Pageant, just across Mississippi Avenue from Convention Hall—was more concerned with this problem than all others combined. Many of the President's principal staff men had come from the home office to set up shop in the Pageant. The chairman of the credentials committee, David Lawrence, the former Governor of Pennsylvania, commuted between the Pageant and his committee in the Convention Hall ballroom. Martin Luther King; Walter Reuther; Joseph L. Rauh, Jr., counsel for the Freedom delegation; Governor Carl Sanders of Georgia; Senator Olin Johnson of South Carolina; liberals, moderates, conservatives; intellectuals and big-city bosses; Hubert Humphrey, who had been assigned to the Mississippi problem while he waited out the Vice-Presidential suspense story—they all met repeatedly at the Pageant. The President himself was a steady participant in the discussions by direct telephone line from the White House.

Everyone seemed to agree that the Freedom delegation had no valid legal claim to the Mississippi seats, but there had to be some symbolic gesture to demonstrate belief in the cause of civil rights. The President, for his part, simply wanted a solution that would leave everybody happy. Seats as "honored guests"—without votes—were offered to the Freedom delegates. They refused them. They were part of a protest movement and they would protest. Keep working on it, the President said, and his negotiators skipped another meal and kept working on it, and the young demonstrators sat adamant on the Boardwalk in front of Convention Hall.

At midday on Monday, the opening day of the convention, I stood there in front of Convention Hall in the midst of delegates, tourists, souvenir salesmen, television cameras and pickets—civil rights pickets, American Nazi Party pickets, "White Party of America" pickets, Women's Strike for Peace pickets, and pickets protesting "school-busing" policies in New York City. The first session of the convention was not until evening, but the Democrats had scheduled so many ancillary entertainments during the day that a man was hard put to decide where to go first to get into the swing of things.

Before I could make a decision, an unscheduled, entirely unofficial riot occurred close at hand on the Boardwalk. A half-dozen scowling young storm troopers, really astonishingly dull of eye, wearing brown shirts and swastika arm bands, marched past with signs denouncing the President. A man jumped out of the crowd and swung at a storm trooper. There was a swift flurry of fists, shouts and thuds before the combatants were buried under a horde of policemen and whooping camera crews.

When order was restored, a large man from Washington, wearing a Johnson button and a fresh bruise on his left cheek, held an informal Boardwalk press conference in which he confessed to having struck the first blow. He said he was not a delegate, merely a tourist, but he did not like Nazis.

"No, they didn't exactly do nothing," he said, "but when I heard one of them say something about 'down with Johnson,' I lost my composure, you might say, that is, I went after them."

Meanwhile, a second large man, this one from Pittsburgh, held another press conference nearby and confessed to his clutch of newsmen that he had struck the first blow. His description of the melee was graphic and, although he did not have a bruise, he said he had a sore fist. From my point of view in the middle of several kinds of excitable pickets, it might have been either of the men, or both, who had struck the first blow. The storm troopers did not hold a press conference. They were all hustled away, still scowling, in a paddy wagon to be charged, a police captain said, with inciting to riot. Atlantic City jurisprudence later settled on disturbing the peace.

Getting back to the official schedule of events, I drove out to the Mays Landing Country Club, where Tony Lema and Sam Snead were playing an exhibition golf match, with the proceeds, after their fees, going to the Democrats. The man in charge of ticket sales said he thought it was the first golf match ever played to raise campaign funds. (The Democrats have come a long way. Try to imagine a Democratic golf match thirty years ago.)

The gallery was not large, many of the Democrats having elected to attend an optional event, the horse races, and there was some doubt in the sponsors' minds that this experiment in fund-raising was going to make expenses. I caught up to the golfers on the fifth hole, a short par-four dog-leg. Snead conferred with his caddie, chose a three-wood, took that marvelous pure swing of his, and hit the ball through the dog-leg into a swamp. Walking down the fairway, I had an opportunity to talk with Snead, and he said, No, he had never heard of playing golf for politics.

"I don't go for either party," Sam said. "I just go one way or the other. Now, Johnson, I'm not sure he plays golf at all. He's a horseman, which is all right if you like to ride horses. Barry, I've known him since before he got to be a Senator. He used to play a lot of golf. But let me tell you what gets me: I asked that caddie back there if I'd be safe with a three-wood and he said sure and here I am in the woods. I wish I hadn't asked him."

The political interview with Snead was over—he came out of the swampy woods with a wedge and got his par four—and the interview with Lema on the next hole was shorter but also somewhat inscrutable.

"I don't ever talk politics at all," Lema said cheerfully, "not at all. I just vote for the guy I want, and this time I don't see anybody I want to vote for, but I don't talk politics with anybody." When I left them at the fourteenth hole, they were both even par and the gallery had grown to more than 1,000 people, probably more than enough to pay expenses, and Lema was striding down the fairway with Senator George Smathers of Florida, not talking politics.

Back on the Boardwalk, I made it to the ballroom of the Shelbourne Hotel in time for a program called "A Musical Salute to President Johnson and Women Doers," featuring Carol Channing, Sally Ann Howes and the New Christy Minstrels. There were about 2,000 women doers in the ballroom, talking, laughing, drinking pink lemonade and looking at their hats in the mirrors on the ceiling. I will not say that the Democratic women in Atlantic City were more attractive than the Republican women in San Francisco, but they were more cheerful than their Republican sisters, who sometimes seemed to have come to parties straight from a harrowing chapter of *None Dare Call It Treason*.

The show, which was produced by David Merrick, no less, was late starting, and Luci Johnson, the younger of the President's daughters, filled time with a little speech. Then she led the rhythmic hand clapping when the New Christy Minstrels banged out a frenetic version of an old song newly entitled "When LBJ Goes Marching In." Miss Channing, of course, was the hit of the day with her song, newly entitled "Hello, Lyndon!" Merrick, the producer of *Hello, Dolly!*, starring Miss Channing, had once offered the song to the Democratic National Committee as a campaign song for 1964, but nothing had been done about it. Then the Republicans took it for themselves as "Hello, Barry!" This woke up the Democrats, who got in touch with Merrick, and he recaptured the song from the Republicans by threatening a lawsuit. Now as Carol Channing lined out "Hello, Lyndon!" the song was worth all the trouble. She sent those 2,000 women doers out onto the Boardwalk humming, and that is always a good sign.

After cocktail parties, poolside parties, receptions, and dinners at such places as Perle Mesta's rented mansion, the time finally came for the Democrats to go into Convention Hall and begin their convention. The hall, the pride of Atlantic City, is a mammoth thing, big enough to contain football games on a full-size field (and no punter has ever hit the ceiling) and big enough for all of the more than 5,000 delegates and alternates to sit in the front half of the hall with thousands of spectators behind them. Including the balconies and press stands, there was room for about 20,000 people in the main hall, and $2,000,000 worth of new air-conditioning equipment actually kept them cool. Considering the commodious rooms under the same roof for the committees, convention staff offices, press headquarters, television and radio studios, and considering the location in the middle of the hotel belt, this mighty home of Miss America may well have been the finest arena for a political convention in history.

One thing marred and mocked the whole arrangement: a massive tower built of metal scaffolding, plywood and blue drapes at center-front of the hall facing the rostrum. The television networks needed an elevated platform to get a good picture of the rostrum, but what they built was not the modest platform on stilts that had seemed to suffice at political conventions in the 1950's. This structure, the Great Tower of Atlantic City, was about the size of a small-town bank, and it was as dramatic-looking as the bridge of a rocket-launching cruiser. It had five levels, in setbacks, and on every level there were big snouted cameras and other infernal machinery. It had lights mounted on it at various angles, lacking only a blinking red one at the top to warn away aircraft. On the rear of the tower there was a balcony, and from the balcony a television camera gazed down upon the luckless and defeated citizens who could not see the convention because the tower was in their way. Among the thousands whose view was blocked were almost 1,000 properly accredited delegates and alternates. If they were close enough to the tower, however, they could watch the proceedings on a television monitor at its base.

It is true that a film projector and a few news photographers occupied space on the Great Tower, but it was the creature and the symbol of television's dominance of the hall, the anterooms, the convention program, and the mood and spirit of the occasion. The Great Tower was ridiculous, and so was the scene around it—the aisles swarming with men with antennae on their heads, men with cameras on their shoulders and portable monitors attached to their armored vests, sound men, producers, directors, walkie-talkie scouts, cable carriers, cable carriers' assistants, consultants to cable carriers' assistants, messengers and coffee-bearers with more elite credentials than the chairman of the convention, all circling and lunging and stumbling over one another in their transistorized tribal hoedown.

The television news fraternity is made up mostly of bright, well-meaning competitive people who work hard to bring the word—the eternal picture—to a vast and eager audience, but restraint is not an important part of the fraternity's creed. When the fraternity built that monument to itself in the middle of the Democratic convention, perhaps some higher authority somewhere (if there is a higher authority than television) realized that something would have to be done about all this in the future.

At eight-fifty-six on Monday night, John M. Bailey of Connecticut, the Democratic national chairman, called the convention to order. As he banged the gavel, two enormous pictures of Lyndon Baines Johnson looked paternally over his shoulder. At the rear of the rostrum a communicator held an open telephone line to the President, who was watching on television at the White House. There was an overture of welcoming oratory, and then David Lawrence rendered an abbreviated report of the credentials committee, which had decided to require a good stiff oath of the Alabama delegation but still had not found a suitable compromise for the Mississippi situation. Lawrence implied some of this in the routine-sounding, ambiguous prose of an old pro, but nobody who had been long away from a television set knew exactly what he was talking about. The program moved on to the fun.

Senator John O. Pastore of Rhode Island—a little man of joyful belligerence, with prominent teeth, a black moustache, black eyebrows, and a fearsome light in his eyes—accomplished something that is always expected but rarely occurs at these conclaves. He made a truly successful keynote speech. The standards are roughly the same as those of college pep-rally orations, but it is a difficult art form.

Pastore leaped at the microphone like a mongoose going after a cobra. He was relentless. He growled, roared and keened. He stepped back and sang high notes, and then he bounded forward howling. His rhythm was perfect, and the hall began to throb with him, and his eyes darted and burned behind his shiny glasses as he slashed the air with his hands and filled it with battle cries and torrents of righteous overstatement. He slew the Republicans. Then he stood over the fallen foe and hissed out the measured syllables: "I say shame!—shame!—shame on all your houses!"

The Democrats cheered him every time he stopped to breathe. At the end, when they were getting limp and glassy-eyed and had begun to wail in a steady storm, he hushed them with a gesture and said, "With all the sincerity of my

soul—I say that God did bless America on that day four years
ago at Los Angeles—when John F. Kennedy said, 'I need you,
Lyndon Johnson.' On November third, the people of America will echo that call, 'We need you, President Johnson.' "

Pastore walked to the back of the platform, and the President was there on the telephone to say it was great.

Tuesday was a day when the Democrats went swimming,
held caucuses at poolside and ordered drinks under their
umbrellas; the women could attend a seminar on "Women's
Challenge in the Great Society," and in the afternoon it was
"Ladies' Day" at the races; the Young Citizens for Johnson
held a campaign seminar at the local high school; there was a
clambake at noon at Margate Beach; Mayor Robert Wagner
gave a party in the Palm Court of the Ritz-Carlton to introduce the new candidate for the Senate in New York, Robert
Kennedy; Mrs. Mesta had a big party—she always had a big
party. Almost everybody seemed to be having a fine time.

Hubert Humphrey, normally the most ebullient man in
the Democratic Party, was not having as fine a time as he
would have liked. He had been up most of Monday night
working on the Mississippi problem, and now on Tuesday he
was scurrying from hotel to hotel, trying to put together
something like unanimous support for a new compromise.
The President in Washington still would not settle for a solution that merely an overwhelming majority of Democrats
could accept; he wanted a solution that 99.44 per cent of the
Democrats could accept, and he wanted them to love one
another while they accepted it. Humphrey still had not heard
anything about the Vice-Presidential nomination, and he had
the feeling that he was expected to bring off this compromise
before he would hear anything. Life is hard in the service of
Mr. Johnson.

The compromise was approved by the credentials com-

mittee late in the day. The Mississippi regulars, like Bull
Connor's Alabama people, would have to take an oath of
loyalty to the party. Two leaders of the Freedom delegation
would be seated in the convention as delegates-at-large with
votes. The other members of the Freedom delegation would
be welcome as honored guests. And the party would resolve
to set up safeguards in the future against racial discrimination in any state's selection of convention delegates.

The Freedom Party delegation refused to accept the compromise; this was still a protest movement. Some of the
Democratic liberals most trusted by the young civil rights
leaders argued that the mature and useful thing to do was to
accept graciously, but they got nowhere with their talk of
party rules and political practicality.

Four of the twenty-four white Mississippi delegates signed
the oath, but the rest refused and headed for home. Fourteen
of the thirty-eight Alabamians signed, and most of the others,
led by Bull Connor, staged an ironic kind of sit-in of their
own in the Alabama seats. A number of the Freedom delegates borrowed passes from friends in other delegations and
infiltrated the hall to occupy some of the Mississippi seats.

The television networks, looking for action during dull
proceedings, covered the sit-ins and seating scuffles so diligently that a viewer could get the impression of a terrible
crisis among the Democrats. On the contrary, the news was
that there was *not* a terrible crisis among the Democrats.
Some reporters and commentators did try hard to keep it all
in perspective while the cameras cut from Connor to pickets
on the Boardwalk, from Freedom delegates in the Mississippi
seats to sergeants-at-arms struggling with somebody (probably a television cameraman) at a barred door.

Speaker John McCormack of Massachusetts, the permanent chairman, talked fast and swung the gavel faster, and

the compromise sailed through on a voice vote. Virtually every influential Democrat in Atlantic City had agreed to it in advance. What was important about the whole interlude was that Lyndon Johnson and his agents had managed to put together something like 99.44 per cent support for a reasonable compromise on the inflammatory issue of civil rights.

There was nothing in the Wednesday-morning papers about Mr. Johnson picking Senator Humphrey for Vice-President. People who had sworn not to be drawn into the President's carefully contrived suspense plot began to be drawn into it deeper and deeper. The top men in the party, the most reliable journalists and the most dignified hotel doormen kept telling one another that it had to be Humphrey, but they were haunted by wispy theories that the President planned some fantastic switch at the very end. A few speculators still were making bets at very long odds on Senators Pastore, Eugene McCarthy of Minnesota, Thomas J. Dodd of Connecticut, Mike Mansfield of Montana, and Edmund Muskie of Maine, or Governor Pat Brown of California, or Mayor Robert Wagner of New York. Those were some of the good names that had been bouncing around for weeks and months, and what kept them bouncing was something they had in common: they were Roman Catholics all. The uses of religious prejudice in American politics had changed so radically in recent years that Humphrey's Protestantism was rather widely regarded as a weakness in his qualifications. Vice-Presidential qualifications, with all the considerations of ticket-balancing, are complicated. Polls showed, for example, that Humphrey was strong in the East and West, very strong in the upper Middle West, but relatively weak in the South. In the South he was better known than the other possibilities but known as a very liberal politician; his colleague, Gene

McCarthy, was not nearly as well known in the South but was preferred there over Humphrey because the southern voters did not know McCarthy well enough to know that he was at least as liberal as Humphrey, and probably more so. When Vice-Presidential seminars turned to such subjects as the probable anti-backlash effect of Pastore's urban Italian-Americanism as against the probable good effects in the West of Mansfield's moderate rural Irish-Americanism or the probability that conservatives in the South and Middle West would be reassured by Dodd's anti-Communist image, some of us tended to get such headaches that soon we could not understand a word that was being said.

Humphrey had received a solid hint from the Pageant Motel late Tuesday that he would be called to the White House to receive the word, and his Minnesota colleague, McCarthy, weary of it all, withdrew early Wednesday. Humphrey got the call later Wednesday—no definite word, just come on down here. When he reached the chartered airplane at the local airport, he found Dodd there, shrugging. Dodd had received a call, too. It was more than a man could worry about any more; Humphrey slept most of the way to Washington.

At the White House the President had been putting on a show that kept many of the newsmen in Atlantic City watching the teletype from Washington rather than covering whatever was going on in Atlantic City. After lunch, Mr. Johnson led a herd of panting reporters on a fifteen-lap, four-mile, ninety-minute walk around the White House grounds. He delivered a rambling critique of the convention (it was a fine convention), lectured on a packet of polls in his pocket (he was beating Goldwater by a landslide), and read from his latest medical report (he was strong as an ox); but he did not disclose his choice for Vice-President. A White House corre-

spondent called his bureau chief in Atlantic City and reported, "He's going around again. Twelfth time. We're
dropping like flies. It's a death march."

When Dodd and Humphrey reached the White House,
Dodd talked privately with the President first. Teletype
printers in Atlantic City pulsed in neutral, and some of the
speculators on Dodd—at odds of fifteen to one and up—
breathed heavily. Dodd came out and said blandly that the
President had sought his advice on a Vice-President. Humphrey went into the President's office a few minutes after six
P.M., and that was when he got the word, although the waiting world still was not told anything. The waiting sign shop
in the basement of Convention Hall did receive information
at six-ten P.M. that caused it to go ahead with a batch of "LBJ
and HHH" signs. The stencils had already been made.

After eight o'clock the President and Humphrey went to
Andrews Air Force Base to fly to Atlantic City. As they prepared to board Air Force One, the President walked Humphrey over to a group of reporters and said, "Boys, meet the
next Vice-President." That was the first public announcement.

Mr. Johnson had consulted Humphrey on the choice of
men to nominate and second the next Vice-President, and the
line-up had been flashed ahead to Atlantic City. On the
plane, the President watched on television while his own
name was put in nomination by Governors John Connally of
Texas and Pat Brown of California. He landed and took most
of the television play as the demonstration began. He talked
with reporters at Bader Field and then drove to the Pageant
Motel while at the convention the organ boomed; two or
three bands played against each other; huge balloons bearing
the names of the states ascended to the ceiling; showers of
of tiny red, white and blue stars and parachutes carrying

American flags came down on the heads of the crowd; pop-guns fired streamers into the air; and hundreds of youngsters carrying their homemade signs churned around the aisles with the delegates. The demonstration went on for thirty minutes, and then there were seven seconding speeches before Lyndon Johnson was nominated for President by acclamation.

Then he was walking out onto the podium in the din, nodding, smiling, his hands moving in an endless series of little waves and benedictions. He would suggest to the delegates whom they might consider nominating for Vice-President. He began, "My fellow Democrats, columnists and commentators . . ." Grinning, dragging out the mock mystery to the end, Mr. Johnson recommended "the man best qualified to assume the office of President of the United States . . . my close . . . my long-time . . . my trusted colleague . . . [and here he paused so long that the convention rocked with laughter] . . . Senator Hubert H. Humphrey of Minnesota!" (He pronounced it 'Umphrey, the old southern way.) The President's choice bounded forward to join him, and there was another gleeful demonstration featuring hundreds of "LBJ and HHH" signs that bloomed from under the delegates' chairs. Even a few of the delegates who were not enthusiastic about Humphrey found themselves cheering him. His own beaming enthusiasm was contagious and, anyway, he had been through so much.

At the height of the celebration for the Democratic ticket of 1964, the ballon inscribed "Alabama" detached itself from the cluster on the ceiling and sank slowly into the orchestra, where the slide trombones knocked it flat after Humphrey was nominated by acclamation.

On the morning of Thursday, August 27, the last day of the convention, the great hall was thrown open to 17,000 young people who had been invited to come and see for themselves the youth and vigor of the Democratic Party. The day before, it had been old people and the program had been Social Security and Medicare. Now it was young people and the program was Barbra Streisand, Vic Damone, Paul Newman, Peter, Paul and Mary, and the Serendipity Singers. Oratorical support was provided by Senator Birch Bayh of Indiana and Governor Ned Breathitt of Kentucky, both chosen because they looked young and trim and knew when to quit orating at young people waiting to hear Barbra Streisand sing. They quit in good time, and she sang, and everyone sang, and Paul Newman said he felt sorry for Elvis Presley and Sandra Dee, who had enlisted with Goldwater. Hubert Humphrey was escorted to the stage, and he made a longer speech than the youngsters probably would have put up with from anybody else.

"Sometimes, you know, a person does feel sorry for the opposition. . . . There is so much good humor here, and the opposition doesn't seem to have any of it at all. . . . Whenever you meet a Goldwaterite, extend the hand of friendship and give him a chance to live a new life. Welcome him into the happy multitude. . . . And remember, we don't boo, we don't ever boo." Humphrey talked on and on, and the audience even cheered him when his lecture wandered somehow into the value of the proteins in dairy products. At the end the band played and Humphrey put on a red, white and blue vest and a funny hat, and he stood there on a temporary night-club stage in a big white spot while a disembodied voice moved that the name of Young Citizens for Johnson be changed to Young Citizens for Johnson and Humphrey. It carried with a roar—after which Barbra Streisand shook the rafters with "Happy Days Are Here Again."   ,

A few blocks down the Boardwalk there was a party in a lower key later in the day. Mrs. Jacqueline Kennedy, soft-voiced and wide-eyed, stood in a receiving line at the Deauville Hotel for the better part of four hours to shake the hands of 5,000 Democrats who filed past in a hush that seemed almost eerie at a political convention. In three shifts the guests at this reception given by Averell Harriman sat in the hotel auditorium and heard Fredric March recite "I Have a Rendezvous with Death" by Alan Seeger. Then Mrs. Kennedy said to each audience, "Thank all of you for coming —all of you who helped President Kennedy in 1960. May his light always shine. . . ."

That night at Convention Hall, the final session of the convention began with a memorial program for President Kennedy. His brother Robert, looking small, sad, and very young, went to the podium to introduce a film called *A Thousand Days*. The applause for him swelled into an emotional ovation that continued for fifteen minutes. It was a proud, affectionate tribute to John F. Kennedy, expressed by clapping and cheering—the only natural way a political convention has of expressing pride and affection—and it was even more natural and dignified than the recitation of poetry.

Robert Kennedy was the symbol up there on the podium, of course, and the reaction he touched off had been anticipated by Mr. Johnson. The convention schedule had been altered to shift the Kennedy memorial from the first day of the convention to the last, when the matter of the Vice-Presidential nomination had been settled.

The twenty-minute documentary film contained somber and happy scenes of President Kennedy's public life, echoes of the muffled drums on his funeral day, and some punishingly poignant moments with the young President and his children. It left the convention emotionally drained. "Hello, Lyndon!" and youngsters waving pennants pumped it up again as the President arrived to listen to Senator Humphrey's acceptance speech before he made his own. The candidate for Vice-President, bouncy and eager for action as always, took the occasion to kick off the Democratic campaign against Senator Goldwater. He cited a list of legislation and policy matters—from the civil rights bill to the nuclear-test-ban treaty—on which "most Democrats and most Republicans in the Senate have agreed." It was a long list, embracing many of the major issues of recent years. And after each citation, Humphrey shook his head and said, "But not Senator Goldwater!" Soon the crowd was roaring the punch line with him, then for him, and the mood in the arena indicated that most of the participants in the speech had got the idea that war on the Republicans was going to be fun.

The President's acceptance speech was a change of pace—for the convention if not for Mr. Johnson. He spoke slowly, often softly, never belligerently. He was in the role he liked best: the father of us all, the philosopher of the Pedernales, the reasonable man offering comfort and guidance to everyone, even Republicans (and no confession of sin would be required). He spoke of vast military power and yearning for peace, of civil rights and an end to disorder, of prosperity's obligation to erase poverty, and he looked ahead to all the things that would be done to create a "Great Society."

As Mr. Johnson left the podium, with the band playing and the crowd whooping again, Harry Reasoner of CBS held out a microphone in a tentative way and the President paused cheerfully for an interview. (He had given an exclusive interview to NBC earlier in the convention; Mr. Johnson likes to keep everything balanced.) Shortly—in answer to Reasoner's question, "Are you afraid of the so-called white reaction or white backlash in this election, sir?"—the President launched into an analysis of what was being called the key issue in the campaign just beginning.

"Yes, we have concern about what you newspapermen have

built up as a backlash by constant repetition," he said, frowning at the organ, which was playing very loud. "I've observed all three networks—about the first question they ask is what about the backlash, and we have the three nationwide polls that you people have bought and other networks have bought —Mr. Roper and Mr. Gallup and Mr. Harris. Then we have a number of state polls and they all show that there is a backlash that ranges from a negligible percentage in a good many states up to an average over the country of, I would say, ten to fifteen per cent of the Democrats, for some reason or other. They may not like the way we spell our names, they may not like how we look, or they may not like some of the programs we pass like taxes or civil rights or nuclear-test-ban treaty or defense bills; but ten or fifteen per cent of them are not going to vote Democratic that claim to be Democrats. . . . But the frontlash . . ."

"You coined a phrase," Reasoner said.

"No," Mr. Johnson replied, "that's one that's been coined, but it hasn't been used much because it hasn't been brought out in the open very much, but the frontlash is the group of Republicans who claim to be Republicans who are not going to vote Republican this year, and that frontlash, according to these same polls, is about two to three times larger than the backlash. So if you're really concerned with lashes, now that you've fairly explored the backlash, let's get into this frontlash, and you'll find about one out of every three Republicans have stated that they are part of the frontlash and they will not vote Republican. . . ."

People were pushing and shoving around him, and the President had to move on. Having managed the convention, directed the Vice-Presidential plot, accepted his party's nomination, and analyzed the coming election for the home viewers, he was off to cut the cake at his fifty-sixth birthday party (it was indeed his birthday, along with everything else) and to see his portrait painted in blazing fireworks above the Boardwalk.

Then, as he said, he would be taking old 'Umphrey down to Texas for the weekend, "and there in the shade of the live oaks on the banks of the Pedernales we'll talk about our duty."

BARRY GOLDWATER's America, autumn, 1964: disorder, disillusionment and moral decay. Freedoms being lost. Military power draining away. Appeasement, softness on Communism, weakness. A bumbling, corrupt, all-powerful government crushing the incentive and pride of the citizens. Criminals roaming the streets, women afraid to go out at night, courts encouraging lawlessness and twisting the Constitution out of its honored shape. Laziness and handouts. Hopelessness and confiscatory taxes. Everyone trying to make everything complicated when everything was really very simple. A shifty, scheming, bullying tyrant presiding over all. The Decline and Fall . . .

That was the premise, anyway, of Goldwater's speeches as he campaigned in September. The assumptions were awesome, the words were strong, and the tone was the tone of a moral crusade to save a country in disgrace. That was how the speeches were on paper, but they did not come out that way. Barry Goldwater said the words, or most of them, but he was somehow bland, detached, even mildly good-humored about it all. His eyes did not smolder. There was not much zeal in him, and sometimes he was nothing less than bored with his own theme. After overstating the problems, he understated the solutions. The Goldwater solutions were mostly general, vague and tentative. In the past his bold, specific solutions had got him branded as a radical, and now as a nominee for President he was full of caution when it came to curing the terrible national ills that he described. He was on the attack, but his mood was defensive.

In any case, he was not making the converts that he needed to make. While he was pleasing the Republican conservatives and gathering support in the South and among the northern backlashers, he was not making headway among the voters in the center of American politics. Many of these people may not have been enthusiastic about Mr. Johnson, but they were not joining the Goldwater crusade. Some were repelled by it, some were afraid of it, and some just thought it was silly.

Mr. Johnson's campaign began slowly and somewhat deceptively. His associates let it be known that he probably would stick close to Washington, concentrating on being a busy President of all the people, as the phrase went. He did work in a Labor Day speech in Detroit. He flew to Florida and Georgia to encourage the citizens after Hurricane Dora, and he encouraged them close up, shaking their hands. He flew to Oklahoma, Arkansas and Texas. And there were other trips and occasions on which a busy President found chances to get out among the people, make some headlines and take a big share of the evening news on television. The President's speeches were about national unity, the good life, peace and nuclear responsibility. Meanwhile, Hubert Humphrey toured the country keeping Goldwater more specifically in perspective; the President's Cabinet members and leading members of Congress answered Republican criticism of the administration.

That much-sought-after phenomenon in Presidential campaigns, "a true national debate," was not developing. The Republicans blamed Mr. Johnson; they said he was afraid to face up to Goldwater on the issues. The Democrats blamed it on Goldwater; they said that he was beating himself on the issues and that some of his positions were so preposterous that there was nothing to debate, anyway. Goldwater himself worried about not getting his message through to people. He worried about it aloud in a speech to the American Political Science Association, which was meeting in Chicago: "Your science is responsible for discovering a psychological principle that is almost as important as the discovery of the wheel, so far as politics is concerned. You call it selective perception. I've always thought of it as filtered listening. People, by and large, let only those things with which they agree get past their filters. . . . During the campaign, which is supposed to be a solemn debate, they turn on the filters and hear only those arguments which bolster their previous convictions."

It was a great campaign for filtered listening, all right. The same impulse, in the form of filtered reading, probably accounted in large part for the incredible popularity of three bad books: *A Choice Not an Echo,* by Phyllis Schlafly; *None Dare Call It Treason,* by John A. Stormer; and *A Texan Looks at Lyndon,* by J. Evetts Haley. The Fair Campaign Practices Committee published a special edition of its newsletter to condemn them all in careful reviews. The Democrats identified all three authors as members of the John Birch Society; the books were recommended by the society's libraries and distributed in many cases by members of the society to bookstores, drugstores and even to local Republican headquarters. The Republican National Committee publicly washed its hands of the books, and most campaign officials at all levels refused to take part in their distribution. Yet these three paperbacks achieved a combined circulation of 16,000,000 copies in the first nine months of the year.

The books comprised an almost ideally filtered reading list for highly emotional conservatives whose ethical standards could be satisfied by the theory that where there's smoke there's fire—and whose imaginations were sufficiently fervid to carry the theory a long step farther: where there's a rumor that somebody saw something that might have been smoke, there's also fire.

The Stormer book, notable for its huge subterranean system of footnotes that often led the conscientious reader into confusion, contradiction and never-never land, was a study of treason in the United States government—"the carefully documented story of America's retreat from victory." The Fair Campaign Practices Committee distributed a review of the book by the National Committee for Civic Responsibility, a nonpartisan organization in Cleveland, headed by the first vice-commander of the thirteenth district of the Ohio American Legion. This review said: "Since this book contains 818 references supposedly substantiating the material contained therein, it gives the appearance of being the well-documented study which it claims to be. Nothing could be further from the truth. . . . In case after case, the author has subverted those references to give a totally erroneous impression and even to say precisely the opposite of what his own reference claims. . . . To the average reader, his documentation seems impressive and few will take the time to discover for themselves that it cannot withstand even the most cursory examination. . . . In summary, the subject book is, at best, an incredibly poor job of research and documentation, and, at worst, a deliberate hoax and a fraud."

As for the Haley book, a good many Americans—for Mr. Johnson, against him, undecided—had nagging questions in their minds about interludes in the President's political and business career in Texas, and there may have been reason to hope that *A Texan Looks at Lyndon* would provide some levelheaded answers. It did not. As the Fair Campaign Practices Committee review (by Robert Sherrill, a correspondent of the Miami *Herald*) said, ". . . An impressive amount of research has been ruined by Haley's hatred for his subject. The result is a book of grotesque perspective, filled with such weird phrases as 'wealthy oil men and other business socialists.' Johnson becomes a 'Stalinist' because he believes advanced countries should aid backward countries. He becomes an atheist because, by initiating the anti-poverty program, he seemingly disagrees with the Biblical assurance that the poor will be with us always. It is a book in which normal actions, seen through a steaming mirage of hate, take on strange and dreadful shapes." A. C. Greene, editorial page editor of the Dallas *Times Herald,* wrote of *A Texan Looks at Lyndon:* "Haley is an historian with some excellent writing to his credit, but he deserts historical principles and takes up personal hatred as his guide. . . . It is so outrageously, surreptitiously wrong that it is almost impossible to isolate the heavy, sick aura of wrongness and define it."

Phyllis Schlafly's book apparently had been written mainly to promote Senator Goldwater's candidacy for the nomination, and it was harder on the "kingmakers" in the Republican Party than the Democrats. William Randolph Hearst, Jr., editor-in-chief of the Hearst newspapers, reviewing the book for the Fair Campaign Practices Committee newsletter, said it was "a monotonous reiteration of purported conspiracies by which, since 1936 and through 1960, Republican Presidential nominations allegedly have been contrived by an arrogant coterie of New York-based 'kingmakers.' " Now, in September, with the kingmakers overthrown and Senator Goldwater finally carrying the conservative banner in the Presidential race (and trailing badly in the polls), this passage from Mrs. Schlafly's book itself was interesting: "One of the favorite tricks of the Democrats is to try to get the Republicans to pass over their strongest candidate and nominate instead a candidate who will be easy to beat." The passage seemed somehow to need refiltering.

There was filtered reading for anti-Goldwater extremists, too, of course. One of the most flagrant examples was a ridiculous and vicious article in a magazine called *Fact*. It was a survey of psychiatrists, by mail, on this subject: "Is Barry Goldwater psychologically fit to be President of the United States?" Full-page advertisements promoting the article appeared in leading newspapers. The American Medical Association, the Republican National Committee, the Democratic National Committee and the Fair Campaign Practices Committee hastened to denounce the whole undertaking, but it was a smear that could not be erased. James A. Wechsler, editorial page editor of the liberal New York *Post*, wrote a review of the article, and it was reprinted in the Fair Campaign Practices Committee newsletter. Wechsler wrote: "A journal with fantasies of virtue that calls itself *Fact* has at last unveiled its psychiatric survey of Barry Goldwater after many days of exhibitionist, egocentric and sadistic promotion. It reveals nothing notably new about Mr. Goldwater; it reveals a good deal about a segment of the psychiatric profession. It is a simultaneous affront to responsible psychiatry and journalism. . . . It must be dutifully reported that 1,864 psychiatrists—14 per cent of those to whom the questionnaire was addressed—felt no inhibitions about rendering an uninformed judgment off the top of their heads. Of those wise men, 1,189 pronounced Goldwater unfit; 675 found him fit." Wechsler said it amounted to nothing more than "vulgar absurdity," and so it did; but the filtered readers and filtered thinkers quoted the survey to one another with solemn satisfaction.

If the campaign had seemed to become somewhat stagnant rather than to take on new life since the conventions, there was hope of better days to come at the end of September. Barry Goldwater was going to make a "whistle-stop" tour. When the train is on the track, and the orator is on the back platform, and the mood of cheerful madness is spreading down the line, then Presidential campaigning has returned to fundamentals and there is joy in politics again. As the travelers assembled in Washington, they reminisced about Harry S Truman, the demon whistle-stopper, and about Thomas E. Dewey, who criticized his engineer, created a terrible labor-relations incident on the spot, and allowed James Reston in the press car to end his story on an inspired note: ". . . and the train pulled off with a jerk." They remembered the "LBJ Special," which swept through the South in 1960, emitting "The Yellow Rose of Texas" with such unimaginable power that cattle were stunned in the fields and votes were shaken out of trees. It was on that trip that the then candidate for Vice-President had confronted a skeptical audience in the railroad yard at Culpepper, Virginia, early one morning and suddenly cast out the classic challenge, "What did Richard Nixon ever do for Culpeper?"

Senator Goldwater's campaign train pulled out of Union Station, Washington, in the rain late on the night of Monday, September 28, beginning a 5-day, 2,500-mile trip to a total of 33 cities and lesser whistle stops in the traditionally Republican heartland of Ohio, Indiana and Illinois. The Goldwater staff considered this perhaps the most important undertaking of the campaign. If the Senator's fortunes were going to take a happy bounce, this was the time for it to happen. The 18-car train, powered by 3 Diesel units, carried the candidate and Mrs. Goldwater, 27 members of his campaign staff, about 100 news people, the customary railroad and diner crews, augmented by a dozen supervisory worriers—and, as it turned out, a female Democratic spy who might have been cast in Hollywood for the Orient Express.

The candidate had made a going-away speech in front of the station to a soaking but spunky crowd and then had climbed onto the back platform of his train to say a few more words of farewell. The loudspeakers failed him right at the start, but he put on a Baltimore & Ohio trainman's hat, blew a whistle, and the train began to roll. On the next track a Pennsy trainman leaned out of a baggage car and yelled, "All the way with LBJ!" Then, as the Goldwater train moved away, the Pennsy man waved and yelled louder, "Have a good trip."

Each member of the press contingent found in his compartment a mimeographed single-sheet newsbill entitled "The Whistle-Stop." Under an attractive red masthead with a line drawing of an old-fashioned train, the message began, "Good evening. We welcome you to our exciting trip. . . . We know that this could be an arduous and trying expedition, and in some circumstances a dangerous one. But in the interests of good fellowship, we have formed a small group whose purpose is to keep you advised, informed, protected, and, with considerable assistance from the Senator himself, amused." Next, a quotation from the going-away speech that the candidate had delivered within the hour: "Living in Washington, and reading newspapers that are solidly committed against our campaign, you might well wonder what's happening out in the real world." The newsbill, speculating on "how far west the real world begins," listed four large Ohio newspapers that had come out against the Republican nominee for the first time since 1936. After assuring its readers that "fluoride has not been added to the water on this train," the newsbill signed off: "Watch for the next edition of 'The Whistle-Stop' at breakfast tomorrow morning." Obviously it was the work of a master spy.

As the train rolled through the night toward Harper's Ferry, reporters gathered in the lounge car plastered with

Goldwater posters to receive from the candidate's press staff a couple of texts of speeches prepared for the next day and to discuss politics and espionage over drinks. It would have been almost impossible not to identify the spy in the company there in the lounge. She was studying a speech text like a responsible lady journalist. She had dark hair that fell to her shoulders, darkly knowing eyes, long lashes: she looked exactly like a spy.

When an opportunity presented itself, I asked her quietly, "Are you the spy?"

"I don't know what you are talking about," she replied— and I was sure.

"How did you smuggle your mimeograph aboard the train?"

"In a violin case," she said, carefully not looking up from her speech text.

Parkersburg, West Virginia, eighty-twenty-five A.M., *Tuesday, September 29.* The train stopped at Parkersburg on this foggy morn to pick up the first shift of Ohio politicians who would ride across the Ohio river into their state with the candidate. There is a traditional order in these things. Politicians of state-wide significance ride the whole way in their state. Local leaders get on one stop ahead of their town, ride in with the candidate and then get off the train to make room for the next load of local heroes.

This would be a long stop in Parkersburg. The first Ohio stop was just across the river, and we were ahead of schedule. With two or three other adventurers, I got off the train and walked along the gravel and cinders to the rear car to see if Senator Goldwater was stirring. He was on the rear platform, alone, in his shirt sleeves, gazing out at the empty railroad yard.

He spoke cheerfully, said he had slept well, and observed

that campaigning by train probably would be more restful than using an airplane except that "you keep taking these local politicians aboard at every stop, and actually this is why both parties have about given up on trains." The candidate is expected to spend some time with each new shift of political passengers, invite the more important ones into his private car for conferences, and generally play the host all day, besides making speech after speech.

A man and woman walked across the tracks with their son, Randy J. Riffle, age five, who was on his way to kindergarten. His parents handed him up to the candidate, who perched him on the railing, held him securely and spoke to him pleasantly, but Randy J. Riffle was frightened of the height and would not say a word. His parents backed away and began to take pictures of Randy J. Riffle and Senator Goldwater. It was a Polaroid camera. They could not seem to get the exposure or something right, and the candidate had to hold the silent, rigid Randy J. Riffle for more than five minutes. The candidate did not seem to be concerned about it and went on talking with the reporters.

Somebody mentioned that the train had no name. In the case of the chartered jet that he was using in the campaign, Goldwater had chosen the name "Yai Bi Ken"—"house in the sky" in Navajo. "We tried to find a Navajo or Hopi name for the train, but it would have been a string of letters about a mile long," Goldwater said. "The closest we could come would have been the words for 'big mule with smoke coming out of it,' and I couldn't go for that." Everyone laughed but Randy J. Riffle. His parents were still fussing with the camera and saying, "Say hello to the next President of the United States, son."

While we paused at Parkersburg, counterespionage activity aboard the train moved swiftly toward a dramatic conclusion. The Goldwater staff had staked out the suspect's compartment—Car 12, Compartment 7—during the night. When the spy emerged at dawn to pad through the swaying coaches, slipping the morning edition of "The Whistle-Stop" into the cracks in doors, she was followed. While she was at breakfast, her compartment was searched and a cache of the newsbills found. (The first two editions had been mimeographed in Washington and brought aboard. The spy's boss, or "control," had arranged to follow the train by plane and car, mimeographing the newsbill and smuggling it to the spy for distribution.) When Victor Gold, the assistant press secretary, confronted the spy, he found it in himself to speak the line, "I think you have made your last delivery, my dear." The spy confessed that she was Miss Moira O'Connor, twenty-two, of Chicago, and not Chuck Cicero of something called the Newman News Service, which was the identification on the press credentials used to purchase passage on the train at Goldwater headquarters in Washington. She had never looked like her name would be Chuck Cicero.

Miss O'Connor, an advertising copywriter, told the press that she had been doing volunteer work for the Democratic National Committee, and she confirmed the widespread suspicion that the mastermind of this caper was the legendary Democratic agent, Richard Tuck, who had managed other schemes to disrupt Republican operations in the past.[1]

---

[1] Richard Tuck, forty, the son of Republicans, was born in Phoenix, Arizona, and claims to have bought his first pair of long pants in Goldwater's department store; but he made a unique name for himself in politics by ingenious, good-natured harassment of Republicans, especially Richard Nixon. In California, where the mysterious Tuck's work became well known in the mid-1950's, he sneaked Democratic signs, balloons and propaganda into Nixon rallies; invaded one himself in a "Nixonette" costume; contrived to scramble Republican travel schedules; hired actors to ask embarrassing questions on the hustings; and once arranged for Nixon to be photographed in Los Angeles' Chinatown in front of a bilingual sign that said in English, "Welcome Nixon," and in Chinese characters, "What about the Hughes loan?" (the loan being an issue that was hurting Nixon at the time). Thanks to Tuck,

The spy, wearing a trench coat and a sporting smile, was escorted off the train in the damp grayness of the Parkersburg railroad yard and left there.

Marietta, Ohio, nine-fifty A.M., *the first whistle stop of the tour.* A band was playing "Everything's Coming Up Roses" as the train eased to a stop in the midst of a lively crowd waving Goldwater signs and signs that said such things as "Barry Loves Bombs" and "Marietta College Students for LBJ." A local Republican official explained to me that Marietta College attracted a considerable number of students from "the East," as if that were all that needed to be said about adverse placards.

After some extremely loud preliminary remarks by Oliver P. Bolton, who was running for Congressman-at-large, and a more modulated introduction by Robert A. Taft, Jr., who was running for the Senate, Goldwater came onto the back platform. "We want Barry! We want Barry!" the crowd chanted. He motioned for silence and said, "I'll tell you something—you've got him." Cheers. "Every time we ask a question of my opponent, the interim President, he leaves town to dedicate another dam," he said. "But I'll tell you something—we have more questions than he has dams." The crowd liked that, and some similar gibes, but the Senator did not pursue the questions or press his advantage to stir up the partisans. In his mild voice, he spoke somewhat defensively of his belief in Social Security and world peace. There was no handshaking, no overt attempt to identify himself with all those

---

Nixon once opened a fortune cookie at a campaign luncheon and found this message: "Nixon for Mayor of Whittier." In the 1964 campaign, Tuck was vaguely identified as a "researcher" for the Democratic National Committee. Prior to putting the spy on the Goldwater train, he had attracted some attention by arranging the release of "LBJ" balloons at a Goldwater rally in Sacramento.

people spread out around him. Standing in the crowd, I had the impression that Senator Goldwater in Marietta's eyes was a remote, shy figure—a famous stranger.

Athens, Ohio, noon of a day that was still gray and misty. As the train slowed down, one of the first signs that slid past the window said "Don't Stop Here—We're Poor Enough." Some youngsters standing on baggage trucks waved "LBJ" signs and booed at the train. Other youngsters nearby waved "Goldwater" signs and booed the press cars. The big crowd included several thousand students from Ohio University, and they were prolific signmakers. One of theirs said, "Even Johnson Is Better Than Goldwater."

"We want Barry! We want Barry!" came the chant. "I'll give you a clue—you have him," came the answer. The candidate spotted a sign in the middle of the crowd: "Help Goldwater Stamp Out Peace." He read it aloud and took it as the text for a long lecture on war and peace. "I remember when I was your age, at the end of World War I, seeing precisely the same signs, hearing precisely the same talk that we must disarm ourselves, that we must become weak because if we are weak then nobody is going to attack us and everybody else in the world is going to disarm, too. . . . Let me tell you young people this—I have been through one war, and that is enough. The surest way to get into a war in this world is to become a weak country, and that is one of the reasons I have been preaching, preaching, preaching the strengths of America. . . . I urge you young people to read your history . . . and find out why we got into World War II, and then sit down and try to explain to yourselves why it is that every time we go to war the Democrats are in power."

The Goldwater fans in the front third of the crowd cheered that last wildly, but few in the other two-thirds of the gathering could hear what was being said. The candidate was speaking quietly, and the loudspeakers on the rear platform were very weak. The warning horn on the train also was weak or inoperative on this occasion. It was supposed to toot three minutes before departure to summon the press back aboard. Whether or not it tooted, the train left fourteen or sixteen reporters—nobody was ever sure—stranded in Athens.

Senator Goldwater, waving from the platform of the retreating train, saw the reporters bursting out of the crowd and running down the track after him. He rushed in off the platform shouting for somebody to stop the train, but it had gone three miles before anybody got word to the engineer. The stranded heroes of the fourth estate, victims of a recurring accident in campaign-train history, scrambled for taxicabs and raced toward the next stop at Chillicothe.

This is probably a good time to note that personal relations between most of the working press—even writers from the wicked East—and the Goldwater staff were reasonably friendly and good-natured. There was constant bantering on the theme that "the press" was anti-Goldwater, but both press and staff managed to keep their sense of humor about it most of the time. The surly mood of the Nixon entourage of 1960, for example, was rarely present in the Goldwater party. (Goldwater kept himself rather remote, and usually avoided questioning by the press, but he was pleasant when encountered casually.)

When the conscientious Vic Gold and other members of the staff moved through the train trying to find out who had been left at Athens, they were routinely accused of abandoning the victims on purpose, and they were given the names of a multitude of "missing" writers, some of whom were typing in their compartments or having lunch in the diner. Told that thirty or forty men were missing, one member of the staff asked incredulously, "That many? But how do you know?" He was informed quickly, of course, "In our hearts, we know they're left."

"You blew the whole thing now, Vic," somebody told Vic Gold. "You left the *U.S. News & World Report* man back there, and David Lawrence is going to be furious." Gold, the steadiest frowner in the modern history of political public relations, grinned for the first time since the train had left Washington.

In the diner, Art Buchwald stood and spoke solemnly, almost tearfully, to a respectful audience: "They were just young kids we sent out there—fine young kids who loved life— fine young kids, and now they are gone . . ."

Chillicothe. The candidate got off the train on a high embankment, escorted Mrs. Goldwater down a flight of temporary stairs, and spoke from a flat-bed truck to a crowd in a park. "We want Barry!" "You have him." Temporary press tables and telephones had been set up near the flat-bed truck—as they must be at every stop on a trip like this—and on the press tables there were stacks of the third edition of "The Whistle-Stop." It said the Goldwater staff feared that the spy incident might not be the last security problem to arise on the trip: "Precautions to protect the Goldwater express have been stepped up. This morning Goldwater staffers were all furnished with identification photos of the James boys and the Younger brothers."

Up on the flat-bed truck, the candidate was making the liveliest talk of the day, so far: "We have an administration that wants to control everyone politically but can't even inspire them morally. We have an administration that talks big but acts small. We have an administration that has a wishbone where a backbone ought to be. . . . I only wish it were possible to engage my opponent in debate, but he is never around the White House enough to find him. In fact, if

Khrushchev calls on that hot line, some beagle is going to answer."

Goldwater told the crowd about leaving "about twelve of our newsmen friends" at Athens, and the crowd snickered, but he shook his head and said he wanted to apologize publicly. "I think we now have it electronically fixed up so that I will know when to shut up, and then they will know it is time to get back in the cars." With that, one element of the new warning system was activated: "The Stars and Stripes Forever" boomed out of the train's loudspeakers up on the embankment. The ensuing charge up the steps, with the more nervous passengers scrambling up the embankment itself, must have made an amusing spectacle for the people of Chillicothe. (The second element of the Goldwater "electronic" safeguard was a walkie-talkie unit with which he proposed to speak directly to the locomotive cab if he saw stragglers running down the right of way in pursuit of the train.)

One taxicab full of heroes of Athens arrived just before the train departed. A second taxicab from Athens missed the train and set out for the next stop at Blanchester.

Blanchester. "We want Barry!" "You have him." The candidate devoted most of his speech to Hubert Humphrey, but he never seemed to be as mad at Humphrey as the Republicans of Blanchester were willing to be. "Hubert Horatio is one egghead who is headed for a great fall. . . . I call him Hubert Horatio Wind. . . . As a talker, he's been clocked at 200 words a minute with gusts up to 325." Flipping the pages of a loose-leaf notebook, Goldwater launched into a random analysis of Humphrey's voting record in the Senate, but there was no shock or horror in his voice, and much of the crowd was restless before he finished. "The Stars and Stripes Forever."

Oakley Station, in the suburbs of Cincinnati, late after-noon. "We want Barry!" "You have him." The candidate spoke briefly from the back platform and then led his entour-age to the long caravan of automobiles and buses that would take everyone to two downtown hotels for the night. Trucks stood by, and there was one of those big transferrings of bag-gage that can never be watched with equanimity; whenever a man parts with his baggage on a campaign trip, he knows, be he candidate or reporter, that he may not get within three states of it again for many days. In the press buses, however, there was peace of mind about another matter that often gives concern on campaign trips: the question of whether the buses will stay close to the candidate. These buses would keep the candidate in view. These buses would not be shunted back in the motorcade by self-important local politicians, governors and the like. These buses would not be detoured by policemen. These buses would not wander into side streets and get lost. All this was true because Vic Gold was in charge of the buses.

Gold, in his way, had become the outstanding phenome-non of the 1964 campaign—a prodigy among bus jockeys, a born master, probably the greatest bus jockey in American politics since buses themselves became a part of political logistics. A bus jockey stands on the steps at the front of the bus, peering through the windshield and talking steadily to the driver. A bus jockey constantly urges the driver to "stay up close, man; come on, man; blow your horn and go." When a governor's car tries to cut in front of the bus, a bus jockey, a good one like Gold, screams at the driver to run the governor up on the sidewalk. When a policeman tries to stop the bus to allow people to cross the street, a bus jockey of Gold's talent does not hesitate to insist that the policeman be run over. Vic Gold's specialty, the measure of his greatness, was his handling of milling crowds that impeded his buses.

Dark, thin, glowering, he would jump out of the door and charge at the crowd, whooping, leaping jerkily into the air, flapping his arms like a strange and dangerous bird. The effect upon the crowd never ceased to be amazing. The crowd would recede as if a bomb had gone off in its midst. The buses would go through, and Vic Gold would swing back aboard his lead bus to acknowledge the applause of his passengers with a quick nod and just the suggestion of a smile.

The crowds that lined the streets of Cincinnati for the Goldwater motorcade were enthusiastic but not large enough to be unmanageable, and Gold had rather an easy time of it keeping the lead bus close to the candidate. He took the opportunity to reel off the pre-hotel logistics briefing, an essential of almost any campaign day. In rapid sequence, he explained such things as that some people would be lodged in the Netherland Hilton and others in the Terrace Hilton but all room assignments and keys would be picked up at the Netherland Hilton; that baggage would be delivered to individual rooms and picked up again in the corridors at six-fifteen A.M.; that the press room, Western Union and telephones had been set up in the Continental Room of the Netherland Hilton, not the Terrace Hilton; that Bus No. 1 would leave the front of the Netherland Hilton at six-forty-five P.M. and stop by the Terrace Hilton on its way to the Cincinnati Gardens for the speech, Bus No. 2 would leave at seven P.M. and would not stop at the Terrace Hilton, and Buses Nos. 3 and 4 would leave at seven-thirty P.M. in the motorcade with the candidate; that Buses Nos. 1 and 2 would leave the Gardens immediately after the speech for the Netherland Hilton, Bus No. 3 would stay behind for half an hour for late filers, and there would be no Bus No. 4 for some reason; that breakfast would be at six A.M. in the Peacock Room of the Netherland Hilton; and that all buses would return to the train, not stopping at the Terrace Hilton, at seven A.M., and anyone who missed the baggage pickup at six-fifteen A.M. should have his baggage on the loading dock of the Netherland Hilton by six-forty-five A.M., and anybody who wanted laundry done could try it on his own responsibility but this was not an official laundry stop—any questions?

Voice from the back of the bus: "Vic, would you run through that again, please, slowly? Do I understand that Bus No. 2 is picking up the room keys or the laundry?"

Gold: "Yes, Don, that's right."

Another voice: "I just woke up, Vic. What town is this?"

Gold: "Toledo."

Another voice: "Vic, Pittsburgh is playing Cincinnati here tonight for the pennant. Try to see it in perspective. Couldn't we run a couple of buses to Crosley Field and you cover the speech for us?"

Gold: "Go ahead, fellows; have your childish fun. I'm fully aware that my function in this campaign is to draw the fire away from the candidate. Go ahead."

The motorcade stopped in front of the Netherland Hilton, where the candidate received an ovation and a shower of ticker tape. In the lobby he walked slowly down a line of Republican workers, shaking their hands as formally as if he were in a receiving line at an embassy. Then he went up for a quiet dinner in his room and a rest before the rally.

The rally—at which Goldwater packed the Cincinnati Gardens with 15,000 fans while the Reds and Pirates, contending for the National League pennant, were playing before 10,000 at Crosley Field—was a howling, throbbing rouser. The crowd was fired up when he came to it, and he had one of the toughest-talking speeches that he had delivered in the campaign.

"The record shows that the interim President doesn't understand the President's job. The record shows that he is not suited for the job. (Applause.) He knows only one thing—to him, running a country means twisting arms and beating heads together. (Applause.) It means buying and bludgeoning votes. It means surrounding himself with companions like Bobby Baker (Boos), Billie Sol Estes (Boos) and Matt McCloskey (Boos). It means turning people into numbers and manipulating them with computers in the White House. It means craving and grasping for power—more and more and more, without end. (Applause.)

"And what about his curious running mate, Hubert Horatio Humphrey? (Boos.) We shouldn't boo him; I just heard him on TV. . . . He said Democrats never boo. Why does this A.D.A. radical of the left want so badly to be a heartbeat away from the Presidency? To drag our nation into the swampland of collectivism? ("Yes!") To bring Red China into the United Nations? ("No!") . . . Look closely, my fellow Americans, at this curious crew who would run your country. . . . What a curious camp!

". . . I charge that this administration is soft on Communism—and you know it. (Applause, stamping feet, prolonged.) I charge that this administration has a foreign policy of drift, deception and defeat. . . . Drift, deception and defeat—these are the watchwords of my opponent and his curious crew." (Applause.)

The crowd was still shouting, clapping and stomping when the candidate left the arena. In the parking lot, a well-dressed woman put her nose close to a window of the leading press bus and screamed, "The press stinks!" A very tired reporter slid the window open and said to the woman, "Boo-oo-oo!" For reasons that were hard to fathom, her face broke into a happy smile and she was last seen waving gaily to the press bus.

The next morning the traveling party and the luggage were reunited with the train and we set out in bright sunshine to traverse the flatlands of Ohio from south to north, from the Ohio River to Lake Erie. After a back-platform talk at Middletown, where the candidate, his traveling companions and the audience all seemed sleepy and dull, we proceeded to Dayton and disembarked for a motorcade to the courthouse square. The crowd was big and enthusiastic. The new sign of the day was "In you head, you know he's wrong." School was out to allow the scholars to look at a candidate for President, and the scholars were competitive. "We want Barry!" one faction would roar, and the other faction would reply, "We want Johnson!" The candidate was caught in the middle, trying to make a serious speech about military aviation. The children kept yelling, and Goldwater finally cut his prepared speech short. He finished with a crack about Bobby Baker and Billie Sol Estes, saying that the New Frontier (in which he tended to include Mr. Johnson) was forever sweeping things under the rug, and "they have so much under that rug now that the New Frontier will have to walk uphill to get to their platform." As the police escorted the candidate to his car, a big detective with a cigar in his mouth said to a loud group of high-school boys on the wall around the courthouse yard, "They shouldn't ever let you punks out of school again, ever."

At Springfield, the next stop, the children were out of school and they were riotous, pushing and shoving and quarreling, jumping and falling off the loading platforms onto the tracks, and generally setting up such a racket that the candidate's speech hardly could be heard by the adults in the front of the crowd. The train's loudspeaker system, to which a couple of big bull horns had been added overnight, seemed weaker than before. Over the chants and yelps and steady rumble of the school children of Springfield, I could barely hear the candidate saying that control of the schools belonged with parents and local school officials.

At Columbus, everyone went downtown in a lunch-hour motorcade. As the leading press bus turned a corner in the middle of the city, a big Manila envelope was tossed into an open window. It was another edition of "The Whistle-Stop," this one containing, along with the usual satirical comment on the Goldwater campaign, a situation-wanted notice: "Attractive young girl. Has Biretta, will travel. Write P.O. Box 008, Parkersburg, W. Va." The candidate spoke from the portico of the Veterans Memorial Auditorium to a crowd of 25,000 to 70,000 people; various local party officials and police officers offered a generous variety of estimates and let you take your choice. It was a big crowd. Goldwater talked seriously about South Vietnam, not calling for "victory," as he so often had before, but lecturing in this vein: "Let me level with you. . . . This has no easy solution. . . . This is a toughie. . . . Some day we could hope and pray we could end that conflict. . . . I have been accused of being a warmonger. . . . I am a peacemonger." The crowd was subdued by the South Vietnam discussion, but Goldwater cheered it up with his sweepings-under-the-rug story and his story about the Bobby Baker dozen: "You know what that is: you get thirteen and kick back two." And he got a big laugh with his line about President Johnson's having so much power that the Democrats "don't know whether to vote for him or just plug him in."

The next stop was Marion, Ohio, the home town of Warren G. Harding. The motorcade from the train moved along shady streets past the Hotel Harding in the faded old business section to a new standard-American shopping center that might well have been in Maine or Oregon. There, on an old-fashioned bare-boards-and-bunting platform in a sea of shiny cars, Goldwater was introduced by a man who would have caused Sinclair Lewis himself to shake his head with disbelief. This remarkable man, full of booster spirit and the joy of Republicanism, made a five-minute speech entirely in rhyme.

The candidate's address was on agriculture, and he began by saying, "I am going to admit something most politicians won't admit—I am not a farmer." In the next twenty minutes, however, he found opportunities to tell his Ohio auditors more about the peculiarities of Arizona weather and plant and animal life than some of them might have wanted to know. The track ran past the shopping center, and the train was to come for all of us when the candidate finished his speech. He finished, but the train did not arrive. Forty minutes passed before it did arrive, and Senator Goldwater spent the time trapped on the speaker's platform shaking hands and signing autographs for a throng of children. School was out in Marion, too.

At Lima, Ohio, late in the afternoon, there occurred an incident known as *The Incident at the D. T. & I. "Y."* In the process of shifting the Goldwater train from one railroad to another, a "Y" on the line of a third railroad, the Detroit, Toledo & Ironton, was to be used to turn the train around and point it in a desirable direction. While all this was taking place on the various tracks, which more or less surround Lima, the candidate and most of the traveling party would go into the center of town for a speech. The usual motorcade met the train on a siding. When the train had been turned and reoriented, it was supposed to proceed to the station in town, near the speech site, to pick up its passengers. It did not work out that way. On a tight curve on the D. T. & I. "Y" the train broke a steam line. An old railroader said that he had "told 'em it would happen, just like it happened to Nixon's train four years ago, but they wouldn't listen." Prolonged repairs were required. When the candidate finished his speech, he and his troop of staff and press went to the station to meet the train, as planned. The train was not there.

While inquiries were being made for the train, somebody looked down a long street and saw the train moving majestically over a crossing, apparently headed out of town. Actually, the train was only shifting its heading on the D. T. & I. "Y." Some of the party pursued the train. Then the group that remained at the station looked down another long street and spotted the train moving around behind the town in another direction. Everyone was told to wait patiently, but the candidate was hustled out of the crowd and taken by car to a siding for an early rendezvous with the train. As it turned out, he was taken to the wrong crossing, and he had to stand around for half an hour signing autographs for a group of children who found him and cornered him against a fence. The train would appear from time to time on one side of town or another, and carloads of passengers would rush off to try to intercept it. Complete confusion. A dozen of Lima's policemen kept rushing from place to place, trying to be at the scene of action if the train and its passengers ever were reunited. Roger Mudd, who found his way to a grade crossing, where a railroad man told him to be calm and wait for the train, insisted that all twelve policemen, in one automobile, sped over his grade crossing twice in different directions. "They were all jammed in there," Mudd said, "all elbows and armpits and revolvers, and when the car hit the bump of the crossing they would all bounce up against the roof, and it was terrible, I tell you, terrible."

The train and the passengers did eventually get together at a crossing. An hour and fifteen minutes late, we sped through the gathering darkness toward Toledo, with Roger Mudd lying on his side on the back of a seat in the press car, demonstrating the perils of a policeman's life in Lima.

Toledo, then Jeffersonville (Indiana) and Seymour, Indianapolis, Logansport and Crown Point, and then Cairo (Illinois) and Carbondale, Centralia, Effingham, Mattoon,

Champaign, Decatur, Peoria, and always "We want Barry!" and "You have him," and the hecklers and "The Stars and Stripes Forever," and on, and on, and on.

President Johnson's campaign up to now had consisted mostly of trips related to his official duties—trips, however, on which he kept happening upon large crowds of voters in important states. He was the evangel of reason, the garrulous persuader, everybody's President with the folksy dignity. Then, on September 28, he added something to an already effective campaign style. He added to it the elemental force of a tornado.

What Mr. Johnson did on September 28 was to attack six New England states and overwhelm them. It was a political trip. He went after the voters frankly, and he went after them in a way that set observers to casting back to Teddy Roosevelt for a comparable example of sheer physical power in campaigning. Traveling by jet and motorcade, he made thirty speeches in twenty hours in six states. (Barry Goldwater on his train in the Middle West made thirty-five speeches in five days in three states.)

The crowds that turned out for the President—in such cities as Hartford, Connecticut; Providence, Rhode Island; Manchester, New Hampshire; Burlington, Vermont; and Portland, Maine—were great, surging, record-breaking tides of people. He plunged into the crowds to touch them, to let them jostle him and tug at his hands and clothes. He stopped his procession to stand on his car and harangue the people through a bull horn. He invited everyone to the Inauguration. When the pushing, shoving crowds tried to break through police lines, Mr. Johnson could be heard shouting in the general din, "Let these people through. . . . Let 'em in closer. . . . Now get out of the way, you cops!" He invited photographers to ride on the "Queen Mary," the open Secret

Service car, and he shouted to them, "Get these crowds, get these crowds!" At the end of those twenty hours his face was lined and sagging in the airport floodlights, his voice was a rasp, and his hands were bruised and bleeding.

With just a month of the campaign remaining, the President had demonstrated how it was going to be from now on. It was said that he was trying to shut Senator Goldwater out of the electoral college by main force. It was said (by Mary McGrory, who almost always senses things right) that he had embarked consciously upon "a program of self-revelation" to counter his wheeler-dealer reputation. It was said that he was giving the people a chance to show their faith in reason, and it was said that he wanted more than victory; he wanted to be loved. Whatever he was trying to prove, he had invested the campaign with new excitement. There was a tornado loose in the land, and it might strike anywhere at almost any time.

As President Johnson increased the tempo of his campaign, he also put his wife to work on the railroad. Mrs. Lady Bird Johnson, who undertook the job with cheer and charm, set out from Washington by train on October 6 for a trip "down home" to the South, where a large part of politics is a mystical exercise in symbolism.

"The Lady Bird Special," spreading southern accents and Dixieland music wherever it went, was the big rolling symbol of an intense but shrewdly soft-sell effort to hold the South for a southern-born President. For southern Democratic leaders under pressure from Goldwater rooters, this was a relatively easy train to climb aboard. After all, who could criticize a governor, a mayor, any southern gentleman for giving gallant escort to a lady, the wife of the President of the United States, traveling in the neighborhood?

Once aboard the train, the local leaders became part of the symbol. The significance of all this was not lost on the voters at the whistle stops along the way. Particularly in Virginia, scene of the expedition's first stops, the voters had been brought up to read the signs and portents for "the word" in politics. Senator Harry F. Byrd, whose organization had dominated Virginia politics from Capitol to courthouse for more than thirty years, had not endorsed Mr. Johnson but, on the other hand, had not "disendorsed" him. In 1952, Byrd came out against Adlai Stevenson, and General Eisenhower carried Virginia handsomely for the Republicans in 1952 and 1956. In 1960, Byrd maintained what was known as a "golden silence," the Democratic organization mostly sat on its hands, and Richard Nixon carried Virginia against John Kennedy. Now Byrd was silent again, but somehow it was a different kind of silence, in which many leaders of the organization at the state and local levels were lining up quietly behind Mr. Johnson. In most cases it had to be a subtle rallying. Goldwater sentiment was strong in Virginia. There would be no headlong rush to the Johnson banner after three elections won by the Republicans with Democratic help. "The Lady Bird Special" was an ideal vehicle to serve as a modest, inoffensive Democratic band wagon in Virginia.

The courtly Governor Albertis S. Harrison and Lieutenant Governor Mills E. Godwin, who was expected to be the next Governor, were aboard the train with Sidney S. Kellam, manager of the Johnson campaign in Virginia and manager, at the same time, of Senator Byrd's token campaign for re-election. Many lesser celebrities of the Byrd organization came aboard and rode into their constituencies. It was a political pageant in a low key, but its significance was understood in Virginia. (If Mr. Johnson himself had ridden across Virginia on the train, that would have been overplaying it, and some of the politicians could not have come aboard. Virginia politics is a web of fine lines seen through a veil of enigmas in shifting light and shadow, with the music of the minuet sounding softly in the background; it is understood only by Virginians and a few outsiders, including, as it happens, Lyndon Johnson.)

Nobody missed the point that this was Mr. Johnson's train, that he was aboard in spirit. Probably nobody would have been greatly surprised to learn at the end of the day in Raleigh, North Carolina, that he had been sitting in the engineer's seat all along. The President was visibly aboard from Union Station to the outlying bedroom city of Alexandria, Virginia. At six-forty-five A.M., he escorted his traveling ladies, Mrs. Johnson and their elder daughter Lynda Bird, to the station and up into the red, white and blue car at the end of the train. Five minutes later, on a day that was coming up sunny and crisply cool, the 19-car train gave a toot of its whistle, emitted a few bars of "The Yellow Rose of Texas" for old times' sake, and departed on its 1,682-mile, 4-day trip to more than 40 whistle stops in Virginia, North Carolina, South Carolina, Georgia, Florida, Alabama, Mississippi and Louisiana.

As the train moved across the bridge over the Potomac, the President joined the first shift of Virginians in the lounge, shook hands all around and said he had a new poll that showed he was leading Senator Goldwater in Virginia. The Virginians, some of whom were feeling a sort of pre-martyrdom for having come aboard this train when they suspected in their hearts that Virginia would go Republican again, were truly delighted to hear the heady talk about the poll. A big crowd, a hillside full of people, was outside the Alexandria station when a blast of "Hello, Lyndon!" announced the train's arrival at seven-ten A.M. Mrs. Johnson, with her husband peering over her shoulder, beaming and counting the house, quickly set the tone of the expedition: "I love the South. I am fond of the old customs—of keeping up with your kinfolks—all of your uncles and aunts and cousins right down to the fifth cousin—of long Sunday dinners after church—of a special brand of gentility and courtesy. . . . I share the irritation when unthinking people make snide jokes about 'cornpone' and 'rednecks,' as if the history and tradition of our region could be dismissed with ridicule. . . . We must search for the ties that bind us together, not settle for the tensions that tend to divide us."

Mrs. Johnson brought up the civil rights question at the beginning of the tour, saying, "The law to assure equal rights, passed by Congress last July with three-fourths of the Republicans joining two-thirds of the Democrats, has been received by the South for the most part in a way that is a great credit to local leadership. . . ." That was the way the President liked to have this touchy issue handled south of the Potomac: accept the responsibility for the new law, but take pains to see that "three-fourths of the Republicans," as against "two-thirds of the Democrats," also accept the responsibility for it.

The President spoke briefly, paying tribute to his wife as "one of the greatest campaigners in America" and mentioning a few of the "basic and radical departures" advocated by the Republican nominee. Then he gave Mrs. Johnson a peck on the cheek and drove off to the office. "The Lady Bird Special" was on its own until sunset, when the President would fly down to a rendezvous in Raleigh for a progress report and a pep talk.

At Fredericksburg, Ashland, Richmond, Petersburg, Suffolk and Norfolk, Mrs. Johnson made her friendly speeches in her soft accent to crowds that grew steadily as the day passed. She always mentioned local history and institutions (something that Barry Goldwater as a whistle-stopper did not always bother with). She was able, too, to attach a relative or an old friend to almost every locality. Mrs. Johnson always cited some points of her husband's record and program; she was proud of him, she said, and she said it disarmingly. The Governor and Lieutenant Governor caught the enthusiasm of the day and endorsed the President warmly. Luther Hodges, the Secretary of Commerce with the reassuring southern accent, took care of such matters as making a point or two about tobacco support prices in the tobacco country. Pretty ladies, the southern wives of members of the President's staff, went out into the crowd at each stop to distribute balloons, badges and pennants. The advance work, which had been planned and directed at the White House as if the President himself were making the trip, was uniformly good. Nothing had been overlooked. When there was a substantial number of young people in an audience, Lynda Bird spoke to them. When she spotted Goldwater signs, she had a little piece she said about the joy of living in a country where you could express any opinion freely, and then she always smiled and drawled, "Anyway, we know in our hearts who's right."

The atmosphere may have been a little sirupy, but "The Lady Bird Special" seemed to be doing an effective job. And it was a happy train. As a matter of fact, "happy hour" was declared on the train while it passed through a thinly inhabited section of northern North Carolina. Throughout the train, politicians, press, hostesses and staff had drinks, olives, little sausages, ham biscuits and cheese crackers. Nobody seemed to remember any precedent for an official "happy hour" on a campaign train, and the general reaction was that whistle-stopping should have been turned over to women years ago.

As the train moved through North Carolina—Ahoskie, Tarboro, Rocky Mount, Wilson, Selma, and on to Raleigh for the night—it became apparent that the "soft sell" could be hardened somewhat in a state with a firmer national-Democratic tradition than Virginia's. The North Carolina Democrats who appeared on the back platform with Mrs.

Johnson began plugging for the President at the top of their voices, and the train began to throb a little. Congressman Hale Boggs of Louisiana, one of the male professionals aboard, had been mild and soft-spoken all day. He began warming up in North Carolina, and by the time the train rolled into Wilson at seven-thirty P.M. he had reached the point where he could roar to a whooping crowd: "Don't let anybody tell you that Lyndon Johnson isn't going to carry the South! He is the first southern President in a hundred years! We in the South are not about ready to turn our backs on him and his lovely lady. Why, he and his wife are as much a part of the South as tobacco and cotton and peanuts and grits and red-eye gravy and you name it, we got it!"

The presence of Lyndon Johnson, which had hovered over the train all day, came down out of the sky in Raleigh, and he was reunited with his wife at a rally in Reynolds Coliseum on the campus of North Carolina State College. There were 12,000 people in the big basketball arena and 5,000 or more outside. It was said to be the largest political rally ever held in North Carolina, and it was a ripsnorter. He made his prepared speech, which was about the Democratic farm program, and then he laid that aside and made another speech, which was about everything. He could not let the audience go until he had told it all about high corporate profits, high wages, the fight against air pollution, the increased freedom and prosperity of most Americans under a Democratic administration, the military power of the country, his efforts at economy in government, his high opinion of North Carolina statesmen, and his conviction that everyone was going to reason together and get along together and love one another.

From Raleigh, the President flew back to Washington before setting out on a whirlwind cross-country trip. Mrs. Johnson moved on toward New Orleans and another reunion several days later. She was booed at several stops in the South, and the publicity was so hurtful to the Goldwater cause that Republican leaders pleaded with their young firebrands to shut up or, better yet, stay home. In the Deep South, civic officials who were for Goldwater made a point in several cases of turning out to greet Mrs. Johnson courteously to set a good example for steaming youth.

Senator Goldwater was on the move, too—in New Jersey on October 7, in Texas on October 8, in California on October 9, speaking in the Mormon Tabernacle in Salt Lake City on October 10, for example. He was bearing down harder and harder on what he called the moral crisis in America, juvenile delinquency, crime in the streets, obscene literature, "erosion of honor and dignity," rioting, and "corruption around our highest offices." Again and again he invoked the Lord, demanded that a high moral tone be set by the Presidency, and spoke up for a Constitutional amendment to restore prayer to the public schools.

Mr. Johnson drew tremendous crowds in the Middle West. He invoked peace, prosperity and moderation, and he cited concern for civil rights and poverty and education as evidence of the nation's sense of moral responsibility. In the normally Republican reaches of the Middle West, Mr. Johnson was exuberant. He had seen the polls, and now he was seeing the people. At the airport in Chicago he shouted, "The Democratic Party, come November, is going to have the greatest victory in the history of America!"[1] The oftener

[1] *The New York Times* said the President's optimism "may have been excessive"; a *Times* survey early in October gave seventeen states and the District of Columbia to Mr. Johnson, with fourteen "leaning" to him. Goldwater was given two states, with eight "leaning." The nine other states seemed to be about even. Two weeks later, on October 23, Republican National Chairman Dean Burch said that a private poll showed Goldwater ahead by 261 electoral votes to 258. If that was the kind of information the Republicans were receiving from their own polls, it was no wonder they did not seem to trust Gallup, Harris and the others.

Senator Goldwater used his hard line about "victory" over Communism, the oftener the President spoke of prudence: "This is no time and no hour and no day to be rattling your rockets." Mr. Johnson's urge for physical contact with the crowds was almost a mania. In a vast throng at Nashville, Tennessee, he yelled at the policemen around him, "Let me near them folks!" Yet he could be quietly and eloquently moving, as he was in New Orleans when he spoke to an audience of his fellow Southerners about civil rights: the law was going to be obeyed, the South was going to summon up its pride and understanding, and the country was going to be whole again. When southern politicians play on racial prejudice to banish all other issues, they are said to "yell nigger." Mr. Johnson pronounced it "Negro," but he talked about it easily and frankly, and he made his point firmly: the era of the racist demagogue was coming to an end, and it was time now for the South to get on with life. The audience applauded.

The Johnson campaign was gathering momentum steadily. Then, suddenly, on October 14, the President received the news that Walter Jenkins, his close friend and associate for twenty-five years, the top man on the White House staff, had been arrested on a morals charge. Acting on anonymous tips, reporters had found the record of the arrest, which had occurred in Washington on October 7, and of a similar charge against Jenkins in 1959. Shortly before the news broke, Dean Burch, the Republican National Chairman, had issued a statement saying there was "a report sweeping Washington that the White House is desperately trying to suppress a major news story affecting the national security." Two prominent lawyers, friends of Jenkins and of the President, had persuaded Washington editors to withhold publication of the story on the ground that it was a personal tragedy without public significance. Both lawyers said they had acted on their own initiative, not for the White House. When a wire service broke the story, it immediately dominated the news. Jenkins resigned and was admitted to a hospital with "nervous exhaustion." The President ordered the F.B.I. to make a "comprehensive inquiry and report promptly to me and the American people." (The F.B.I. reported on October 22 that it had found no evidence that Jenkins had "compromised the security or interests of the United States in any manner"; further, there was no evidence that Mr. Johnson or the late President Kennedy had been informed of Jenkins' arrest in 1959.)

Senator Goldwater said that he would not make an issue of Jenkins' personal conduct but that the security aspect of the case would be a proper subject for discussion in the campaign. This aspect, arising from the vulnerability of morals offenders to blackmail and coercion, promptly became a prime subject for other Republican orators. The Jenkins episode, logically or not, seemed to have given tremendous force to the Republican campaign theme that "moral laxity" and corruption at the top of the government were promoting "moral decay" throughout American society.

What may have been developing as a major crisis in the campaign was dulled and obscured as quickly as it had arisen. Within eighteen hours of the disclosure of the Jenkins arrest, Nikita Khrushchev was deposed as head of the government and the Communist Party in the Soviet Union. Within another eighteen hours came news that Communist China had exploded its first atomic bomb. Momentous events abroad—full of doubt, danger and foreboding—drove the Republicans to the wall again. In prime time on all three television networks, Mr. Johnson spoke somberly to the nation as its cool, experienced and prudent President. "The key to peace," he said, "is to be found in the strength and good sense of the United States of America." The speech was carefully nonpolitical. As most observers also hastened to point out, it was one of the most effective speeches politically of recent times. The central issue of the campaign again was the widespread fear that Barry Goldwater was a dangerously impetuous man.

And that was how it went through the last weeks, the Democrats talking about prudence vs. recklessness, and the Republicans talking about a pure heart vs. moral decay. It was at times a thoroughly dismal business. Probably it could have been worse. At least the Democrats had quit showing their television spot of a pretty little girl picking daisy petals in the sunshine while a grim voice counted down—5, 4, 3, 2, 1—to a nuclear explosion, and Senator Goldwater had publicly repudiated a Republican morality film that blamed lax Democratic leadership for civil rights disorders, dirty books, gambling, topless bathing suits and sin generally. Although the film was being promoted by a Republican front with the noble name of "Mothers for a Moral America," Goldwater dismissed it with disgust as "nothing but a racist film" and it was not shown nationally on television as planned.

The morality issue was particularly oppressive when it was argued not by politicians but by zealous philosophers at cocktail parties, around water coolers at the office, and in the letters columns of the newspapers. Some Democrats denied indignantly that the country had any ethical problem beyond the lack of ethics of the Republicans, of course; anyone who mentioned Bobby Baker's mysterious manipulations was a smear artist; anyone who worried about some of the implications of civil disobedience was a racist; anyone who used a complimentary adjective about Barry Goldwater was a bomb thrower. The self-righteousness of some of the Goldwater fans, on the other hand, was suffocating. They might not have begun the campaign as fanatics, but now in their feverish and sometimes oddly gleeful crusade against immorality they snatched up an assortment of facts, half-truths, innuendoes, fears and gossip and they balled it all up into an all-purpose issue; apparently it was supposed to supersede the whole list of issues involving a choice of radically different approaches to the Communist bloc, nuclear-weapons control, the United Nations, civil rights, Social Security, education, poverty, the domestic economy and the rest. It was the kind of campaign in which a fine, moral example of American womanhood could say to an acquaintance, "How can you *not* be for Goldwater? Where is your integrity?"

That is how it was in the stuffy pockets of morose political discussion. Out on tour with the candidates, however, life was better. It was a frantic, weary, eternally surprising way of life, with the crowds yelling and the big jets screaming and the candidates saving the world in hoarse and broken voices, and time was out of joint and geography did not make sense any more. But it was not stuffy. Maybe crazy, but not gloomy.

It was Sunday, October 25, and the temperature in Fort Lauderdale, Florida, was eighty-three degrees. The press plane landed first, as always, and then half an hour later, at four o'clock, Air Force One came in low and fast against the pale sky. Silver, white and blue, with "United States of America" lettered above the long row of round windows, it taxied quickly to a point directly in front of the crowd, turned slowly in a quarter circle and stopped. When the engines died, the ramp was rolled out and two Air Force guards and a Secret Service man hustled down the steps. The President was in the door. The Stranahan High School band hit "Hail to the Chief," and the President gave a quick little wave. Then, squinting and solemn, big Texas hat in hand, he came down the steps with a fast, side-winding shuffle.

He moved along a receiving line, shaking the hands of the Governor, Senators, Congressmen, state legislators, local

Democratic leaders, and, at the end, a family of Seminoles in costume. He picked up the smallest child, a tiny girl, kissed her on the cheek, and set her down. His right hand went into his pocket, and he counted out the right number of "LBJ" pins and gave them to the child to distribute to her brothers and sisters. He whirled, got his bearings, and walked toward a roped-off area where most of the reporters and photographers were standing. He walked looking at the ground. He stopped at the rope and said to a photographer from Washington, "Hi, George. I'm glad to see you out here working on a Sunday." He shook George's hand. I was behind George writing in a notebook. When I looked up again, the President was standing perfectly still, looking at me without expression. I said, "Good afternoon, sir," and he nodded ever so slightly but continued to stand there expressionless. Then I knew what was expected of me; I had read it in a piece by Richard Rovere in *The New Yorker*. I shifted the pencil to my teeth and held out my right hand. He shook it firmly, started a smile, stopped it before it did more than agitate the corners of his mouth, and settled for a wink.

The President spun away from the rope and took time to look at the crowd for the first time. He surveyed it carefully, rubbing the back of his hand across his mouth. His eyes were half closed. Actually his eyes are always half closed; some people think it makes him look vaguely sinister, but that is the way his eyes work, never wider than half open. With two Secret Service men, he walked very fast, looking at the ground, to one end of the airport fence. Then he pushed the Texas hat to the back of his head and went to work.

He moved along the fence from left to right, his right hand thrusting ahead, grabbing outstretched hands, sometimes two at a time, his left hand moving in quick circles, touching any hands that the right hand missed. His eyes darted around in the crowd too fast to follow, meeting a pair of eyes, another pair, another pair. He was winking and nodding all the while, and he was greeting those people individually, several every second, with his hands and his eyes. Now and again he would stop and say a few words to a child, a giggling woman, an old Negro man whose steady eyes had stopped his own. He passed out "LBJ" pins to some of the small children. The band was playing, and the sound of the crowd followed him in a wave. The people, five or ten deep, were straining against the fence. He stopped, put his hands on his hips and said, "Hey, you folks just push back there a little. You're mashing these little kids." He came to a group of teen-agers thrashing and fighting for front positions at the fence. He stopped and stared at them silently. It was the look of the old Texas schoolteacher, and the youngsters subsided. When they had become unnaturally, almost eerily docile, the President carefully shook each hand and winked and nodded at each youngster. One boy, far back in the crowd, attracted the President's attention, and Mr. Johnson stretched so far across the fence to reach the lad's hand that a Secret Service man made a move to hold the bottom of his jacket to keep him from toppling over into his fans.

When the President reached the end of the fence—it was a short one—after doing 150 yards in about 6 minutes, his car was waiting behind him on the taxiway, with the Secret Service's "Queen Mary" and the rest of the motorcade strung out behind. He gave his little wave to the crowd and stepped into the car. Up ahead, the motorcycles grumbled and roared and led the way out of the airport.

A military helicopter with a blinking red light zigzagged at low altitude in front of the caravan as it sped through the scrubby flatlands of south Florida, past cattle grazing among short palms and cypress stumps, toward Boca Raton.

The President was going to dedicate Florida Atlantic University, a new state institution built on an old federal airport. It was an outdoor ceremony, and a crowd of about 10,000 people was waiting for him. Two airplanes, one pulling a banner that said "Barry Goldwater" and the other pulling a banner that said "Union Labor for Barry," had been chased away by the helicopter, and everything was ready for the President when, wearing a robe and a mortarboard with a gold tassel, he marched in the academic procession to the platform.

Mr. Johnson dedicated the institution and received the degree of Doctor of Humane Letters before the dedication had got cool. Then he made a speech. He talked for a long time about education, deserting his prepared text and improvising.

"I think we just must not rest until each child, GI or no GI, boy or girl, rich or poor, has the opportunity to get the kind of education that he needs and that his country needs for him to have in order to defend it. And I think it is a little wiser policy to do a little better planning, to take the boy out of the cotton field and train him in his normal high-school years and his college years to develop himself, rather than to issue an emergency order and jerk him off overnight and send him on a train to a boot camp and then try to teach him how to fire a missile or handle a B-52 over Moscow without much notice."

He rambled on and on, but he held the crowd's attention. At the end, he gradually picked up his tempo, which had been almost painfully slow, and in the final passage of the speech the words were tumbling out as he strained forward across the lectern: ". . . So I implore you to recognize before it is too late that while the Soviet Union can put up Sputnik I, and while we are debating about it, Sputnik II is saying 'beep, beep, beep' in the sky—that we are sometimes mighty

slow to start but mighty hard to stop. We don't need argu-
mentation about the desirability of preparing our children to
think and act with judgment. But, remember, whether it is
the man that picks up the telephone on the end of the hot
line that is calling from Moscow, or whether it is the man
that sits there with the responsibility of his thumb close to that
button [here he held up his large right thumb for the crowd
to see], that no man's judgment on any given question is any
better than the information he has on that question. And he
can't get all the information he needs in this space age hunting and fishing. He can't get all that he needs on the football
field or the baseball diamond. He has to get it in grade
school, high school, in college, in graduate work, because
Americans must never be second to anyone."

The motorcycles were fired up again. The blinking helicopter swooped in close and beckoned the Presidential procession in a great circle around the new college buildings
toward a sunset of outrageous pink and gold and then another ninety degrees beyond the sunset to the neon glow of
Miami on the dusky horizon.

After a brief stop in Miami, the President flew north to
Orlando. Air Force One landed at McCoy Air Force Base
near Orlando at 9:20 P.M. in a heavy rain. The public had
not been allowed in the area, and the President had only a
few official hands to shake as he was conducted to his car by
an umbrella bearer. Six sputtering motorcycles clustered
around the car. The Secret Service detail, putting on raingear
in the topless "Queen May," looked like a whaling crew in an
open boat. The procession of motorcycles, cars and buses was
a ghostly, surrealistic parade of long shadows in the floodlights and shimmering reflections on the rainy pavement;
somewhere up ahead a siren wailed steadily in the down-
pour.

The motorcade picked up speed as it swung off the taxiway

of the airport onto the connecting road to the main highway. Then the President saw the people standing there in the rain, five deep, ten deep, on both sides of the road. His car stopped. He got out slowly and stood in the middle of the road buttoning his white raincoat. Then he tipped the hat back on his head and began.

Shaking hands, touching hands, nodding, winking, he moved through the rain in the glare of his car's headlights. The crowd was whooping. Photographers stumbled backward ahead of the President, and a Secret Service man walked ahead of the photographers to warn them of obstacles; it would not do for them to fall and pile up in front of the President. A Secret Service man walked at each elbow of the President, fending umbrellas and placards away from his head. Farris Bryant, the Governor of Florida, joined the squad of policemen and Secret Service men trying to keep the crowd on the other side of the road from closing in and swamping the President. The Governor had no raincoat and he was soaked, but he was grinning as he trudged along. Soon everyone was grinning. You had to laugh or cry out there in that driving rain with the President, walking in the middle of the road now, leading the motorcade on foot, shaking hands on both sides.

For a third of a mile he walked through the rain and the milling people, and then he finally ran out of people in the black Florida night.

Next morning at the Cherry Plaza Hotel in Orlando, the President went down to a private dining room to speak to a gathering of Florida Democrats at breakfast. He told them about their senior Senator, his friend Spessard Holland. "Spessard is very serious about spending money any time," Mr. Johnson said. "He is a great man for economy. He does loosen up a little when it comes to spending money in Florida. He came to see me the other day, and he got another eighteen and a half million dollars for Florida, and then he went out and made a speech on economy right out there in front of the White House! Spessard Holland is a great Senator and a great friend of mine."

The President went out into the warm, sunny morning to drive in the inevitable motorcade to a shopping center to make a speech. There was a band in front of the hotel to play "Hail to the Chief" and "Hello, Lyndon!" and the big crowd along the street was in a good humor. So was the President. He decided to walk at the head of the motorcade. He had enjoyed it in the rain; why not do it again on this golden morning? So he walked and shook hands, and the crowds applauded, and small boys ran along beside him at the curb, darting in and out among the policemen to grasp his hand. He saw two boys on the sidewalk with Goldwater signs, and he veered over and shook their hands. Everyone enjoyed that. The boys ducked back through the crowd and ran ahead. He saw them again and shook their hands again.

To the great expanse of people at the shopping center, Mr. Johnson said at the end of a rambling speech, "I say it is your duty, it is your obligation, you do it for yourself, when you go to the polls November third and vote for peace—vote for space—vote for prosperity—vote for Flordia to be one of the fastest-growing states in all the nation, in all the world!"

Then he lowered his voice and spoke softly, slowly, his face close to the microphone: "When you select the man as your President to lead you, you want to select the person who loves peace and has the knowledge, has the experience, and has the desire to achieve it." He held up his right thumb and looked at it, and the crowd was very quiet. "When you select your next President, the man who must sit there with his thumb close to that button, the man who must reach over and answer that telephone, that hot line when Moscow is calling . . ."

At noon the President was in Jacksonville. From the airport the motorcade passed through slums, a Negro neighborhood, on its way to the business district. The porches of the old houses were decorated with "LBJ" posters, and the school children in their Sunday clothes were lined up along the curb. They jumped and squealed as the President's car came down their street with all those motorcycles. Behind the children, on the sidewalks and the slumping porches and in the dark doorways, the older people waved, but they also made a point of clapping very hard and very seriously. They were saluting a southern white man in a big black car, and some of them had never done this before in all their lives.

Mr. Johnson was to speak in Hemming Park, a square of green with palms, stone benches, a Civil War monument and a round bandstand, in the center of the city. He went into a little building at the edge of the park while the local master of ceremonies talked to the crowd. There was a large, loud and surly claque waving signs—"LBJ—Lyndon Baker Jenkins"—in the center of the crowd and another like it, chanting and booing and pushing against the fence near the little building where the President was waiting. The pro-Johnson majority in the crowd was not overly tolerant of the troublemakers, and there were several flurries of shouting and scuffling. The Secret Service did not like the look of the situation, nor did the local police. After much coming and going of security men in and out of the door to the little building, the policemen were told to stand back from the fence when the President came out. The fence ran in front of the crowd from the building to the bandstand where he would speak. The President came out alone, except for one Secret Service agent several paces behind him. Mr. Johnson stopped close to the fence and looked for a moment at the clutch of hecklers nearest him. Then he walked slowly, close to the fence, to the bandstand. The crowd seemed to be under better control from the moment he appeared.

When boos and catcalls broke out during the President's speech, some of his defenders in the crowd set up a racket of their own, and there were angry exchanges between the factions. "We must stop this business of quarreling with each other," he said sharply, and he undertook then and there to convert the hecklers, telling them about the American way and reasoning together and the thumb on the button. Conversions may have been nil, but the ruckus was quelled by the sheer persistence and persuasion of this man who would not pause long enough to be booed. When Mr. Johnson began again on his prepared text, most of the school-age hecklers left him alone. There were some young men, though, with dull eyes and long sideburns, and soon they began to encourage one another in booing and bellowing. Mr. Johnson finally turned to them and said, "I want to greet some of these people over here with another philosophy. Nearly every meeting we have, they send some of their children over . . ." That did it. The word "children" seemed to deflate the young men with the long sideburns; they muttered while the crowd laughed at them for the first time. The President looked happy for the first time, too, and said he would look forward to the day when his friends with another philosophy would "get over their bad feelings and join us."

At Warner-Robins Air Force Base near Macon, Georgia, the Presidential party found a relaxed, happy crowd, and Mr. Johnson shook so many hands that he had to stop and put on a Band-Aid. He kissed several little children. He found a baby asleep in a stroller against the airport fence, and called to Senator Herman Talmadge and Congressman Carl Vinson to come and look: "I've already put one to sleep over here." A pretty woman asked the President if he ever kissed grown ladies, and he said he did in Georgia. He kissed her on the cheek.

Macon was the home town of Rufus Youngblood, the Secret Service agent who had been at Mr. Johnson's side since the day in Dallas when he had pushed Mr. Johnson to the floor of the car and covered his body with his own. As the President moved along the fence shaking hands, he stopped several times, asked people's names, and then solemnly introduced them to Youngblood. Leaving the air base in the motorcade, the President saw perhaps a thousand people standing on a gentle green slope a hundred yards or more from the road; apparently it was somebody's idea of security to keep them back that far. Mr. Johnson stopped the motorcade, got out of his closed limousine and climbed into the back of the "Queen Mary." With the President standing up in the back, pointing at the people and urging the driver on, the big open car took off cross-country and delivered Mr. Johnson to the citizens.

After this side trip, the caravan drove on to Macon, where the President spoke from a platform erected over the City Hall steps. The crowd was huge and cheerful. Standing there in front of the old building that had been the temporary capital of Georgia under the Confederacy, Mr. Johnson spoke of Robert E. Lee, and then, smoothly and easily, he was speaking of Abraham Lincoln and a vision of unity.

"There are still those who are trying in this election to play the politics of diversity, of division. . . . I say when you divide your country, that is wrong. . . . What Americans want today is a new politics, a politics of national unity, a politics concerned with progress and peace for the nation, a politics of honor, and a politics of decency for all. And when the returns come in one week from tomorrow, America will know, and the world will know, that in this land of the free there is no North, no South, no East, no West. . . . There is only one nation, one people, one flag, one Constitution, united and indivisible under God. . . . One hundred years is long enough to burden down our future with the divisions of the past. The time has come—the time is now—to bind up our wounds, to heal our history, and to make our beloved America whole again."

Surely this was Lyndon Johnson at his best. It was his mission to stand there in front of that Confederate shrine in Georgia and say that a hundred years was long enough.

It was just as much a part of him that with his next breath he was drawling a plea to his audience to "take your uncles and your cousins and your aunts" to the polls on November 3 to decide "whose thumb you will put close to that nuclear button, whose hand you want to reach out and pick up that hot line when Moscow is calling. . . ."

The President's press party traveled in a chartered jet that always took off and landed ahead of him so as not to miss the airport receptions. From Macon the press jet took off before everyone was seated—it often happened when we were running late, which was almost always—and people grabbed for the backs of seats or even sat down in the aisle in the rush of acceleration on the runway. A Pan American stewardess was propelled down the aisle, running to keep her feet, and she executed a remarkable leap into the laps of two startled German correspondents as the jet took flight. It was four-twenty P.M. and nobody had had lunch. We would be in the air about twenty-five minutes before landing at Augusta. The stewardesses grabbed things out of the galley and served them more or less at random—sandwiches, peanuts, cupcakes, coffee, cocktails. I got chocolate ice cream and a bottle of beer; that was my lot and I accepted it.

Soon typewriters were tapping and somebody was snoring. A mimeograph in the forward compartment was grinding out transcripts of a speech somewhere back down the line. Two photographers were arguing bitterly about some feud known only to photographers. A radio man was playing back a tape of the President's speech at Macon, or maybe it was at Jacksonville, and the President had his thumb on the button again. The two German correspondents were in the aft galley teaching a German folk song to a stewardess who was mixing drinks. A man typing a story in his lap exchanged seats, losing only a beat or two, with a distinguished columnist so that the distinguished columnist could play a game of gin with his neighbor. A television reporter was saying in loud, well-formed tones to somebody that he didn't care what New York said—he could not make a great deal of sense into a microphone in a driving rain on the back of a moving truck. The rain at Orlando had been too much for him; he was distraught. Friends threw peanuts at him to settle him down.

We were passing through a frothy white cloud. A television cameraman looked out and said, "Think about it: there are three other crazy groups like this out there somewhere, flying around just like they were crazy. It's all crazy. I've decided Miller is the best one to travel with in a way. He stays on the schedule, you know? He sticks to the text. You can mark it and shoot when he comes to it. He makes those speeches and they're rough as hell, but when he gets back on the plane all he wants to do is be happy and play some bridge, you know? He doesn't draw much of a crowd and there's no trouble. Miller is a kind of a rest, you know? But it's all crazy."

An assistant press secretary said over the loudspeaker that the President would be going to Boston the next day and then on to Pittsburgh and Evansville, Indiana, and Albuquerque and Los Angeles. Then he said we were about to land at Bush Field, Augusta. "Please use the forward door only. This is a one-ramp town." Stewardesses and passengers in the aisle ran for seats. The plane landed, as Russell Baker has written, "in a shower of peanuts." It was a good landing and everyone applauded, as is the custom on press planes. Then we all went out the forward door because Augusta is a one-ramp town.

Mr. Johnson spoke in front of the gleaming, new white-marble municipal building, whose wings on either side made a sort of sounding box for his voice. The crowd filled the square in front of the building and filled the street a block away in front of the gabled and turreted homes of old Augusta. "Big crowd, very big," a Georgia editor said, "but a lot of these people are just wrestling with the idea of voting for Goldwater."

"I know the burdens the South has borne," the President said. "I know the troubles the South has seen. . . ." He was interrupted by a band of young hecklers bobbing their Gold-water signs in the twilight and chanting, "We want Barry." He let them drown him out once, twice, three times. After Jacksonville, it seemed strange to some of us that he did not pause and deal with them. But he did not. He let them interrupt him with boos again, and he stood there looking helpless to continue while the youngsters yelled louder. He let the embarrassment of the adult Georgians become something almost tangible.

Then he pointed a finger at the noisemakers and leaned forward on one elbow, close to the microphone. He spoke so softly that everyone, including the hecklers, had to strain to hear what he said: "I think it is better to use the head and the heart than to use the tongue and the voice. I know when you see people, as you have seen them at some conventions when they don't want other people to talk, when the Governor of a great state is not even permitted to speak to his own convention because others would interfere, or when the President of your own country would be stopped and interrupted while he was trying to talk to you in your own land—can you imagine what kind of leadership that would be for the world if that were practiced?

". . . I was always taught as a little boy when people didn't know any better, and when they made mistakes, and when they were rude, and when they didn't show good manners, to turn your other cheek and say, 'Dear Lord, please forgive them, for they know not what they do.' And I think that is the way that the people of the fifty states are feeling. We don't feel hurt, and we don't feel angry. We just feel sorry. And I think that on November third they are going to feel sorry, too."

The crowd cheered and the hecklers were silent, but the President would not ease up on them. It was dark now and the lights in front of him cast a huge shadow of his head and the movements of his hands on the façade of the building behind him. "I was in an election campaign four years ago," he said, "and I returned to my home state in the last days of that campaign. We went to the hotel to wash up before we went to a luncheon meeting, but the entrance was blocked and the hecklers were there, and they harassed us and they hounded us and they knocked my wife's hat off, and they spit on us and they called us traitors and they called us treason artists, and they had ugly signs and they dealt not in a single issue that we were debating. They had only to talk about personalities and little petty things because they were little petty people. . . . It took us more than an hour to walk across the block because of the chants and the saliva that was running out of their mouths and, really, some of them were diseased. . . ."

When he finally looked back at the text before him, he decided to talk for another twenty minutes, and it was only to cheers.

Driving from the airport through the outskirts of Columbia, South Carolina, the motorcade passed a little girl, about ten years old, standing alone under a streetlight with a sign that said, "Hi." That was all it said. It was something, come to think of it, that you saw every day or two on campaign trips: a child, alone, with a sign that said "Hi." I remembered one, an even younger child, a very small boy, sitting on a pasture fence in south Florida with a sign that said "Hi." I had a note of another one, a little girl, holding up her sign in the weedy yard of a ramshackle house beside the railroad track in Ohio when the Goldwater train went by. Perhaps because a man can be overly sentimental when he is tired and away from home, I wondered if the candidates saw those lonely children and appreciated their simple, wistful greetings.

Toward the center of Columbia, the street crowds swirled over the curbs and the President stopped and bull-horned 'em, as the saying went. That is, he got out of his car and climbed up on the rear deck, which had convenient handholds, or even up on the roof, and spoke. He told them that he was glad to see them and that November 3 was going to be a great day, and he urged them to "come to the speakin'."

The crowd at the speakin' was the largest ever assembled in Columbia—somewhere between 40,000 and 70,000, according to local police and newspapermen. It was an almost self-consciously polite crowd that gathered in front of the capitol of South Carolina. Mrs. Johnson had been booed when she passed through on her train; now, however, the civic pride of Columbia apparently extended even unto the most avid Goldwater fans, for everyone obviously was determined to be hospitable. The President made it easy for them. He was hoarse but in good form; he was not ponderous or even very partisan.

After he had talked for about half an hour, he said, "Well,

I will tell you a little story before I go home. This happened down in my country. We lived out on a cotton farm when I was a boy, and we had a little boy there that left a little after lunch one day and went over to the Old Settlers' Reunion, the old Confederate reunion, and he didn't come back until dark that night, just about weighing-in time, just about the time we were unloading our sacks and weighing in. And the boss said, 'Where in the world have you been all afternoon?' He said, 'I have been over to the old Confederate reunion.' The boss said, 'What did you do all afternoon at the Confederate reunion?' The boy said, 'Well, I listened to a United States Senator make a speech.' The boss said, 'Well, the Senator didn't speak all evening, did he?' The boy said, 'Mighty near, mighty near.' The boss said, 'Who was the Senator and what did he speak about?' 'Well,' the boy said, 'Boss, his name was Senator Joseph Weldon Bailey from Texas, and I don't recall all the Senator talked about, but the general impression I got all afternoon was that he was recommending himself most highly.' "

The President said, "It is naturally to be assumed that I would recommend myself most highly." After recommending himself fairly modestly for another five minutes, he said good-by and started home. At nine-twenty-five P.M. we were airborne, and at eleven o'clock the white shaft of the Washington monument was in sight. In the back of the plane, the stewardesses were leading a chorus of "Auld Lang Syne." It did not make much sense really; most of the same people would be back aboard the plane the next day for the run to Boston, Pittsburgh, Evansville, Albuquerque and Los Angeles.

Next night, another airplane. The lights of Lexington, Kentucky, were visible below. Senator Hubert Humphrey, the ebullient, combative, talkative Democratic candidate for

Vice-President, was approaching Blue Grass Field for an airport rally that had been scheduled for midnight. His plane, "The Happy Warrior," was half an hour late, which was not very late when one considered how much ground the Humphrey party had covered during the day. We had spent the morning in the Indian-summer weather of Washington; the early afternoon in foggy New York; the late afternoon in chilly Charleston, West Virginia; and the evening in rainy Cincinnati.

Humphrey had started talking in earnest when he stepped off the plane at La Guardia Airport at noon, and he had been talking more or less steadily ever since—never repeating himself, never putting two dull phrases together, never losing his enthusiasm. Talking on the plane, he was even enthusiastic about hecklers. He said Republican hecklers were turning into one of the biggest assets the Democrats had in the campaign: "I can't believe how lucky we are." The New York press met him at the airport and asked him what he thought of Senator Goldwater's statement the night before that the Republicans would carry New York.

"Oh, did he say that?" Humphrey said. "If the Senator thinks he is going to carry New York, he can't be using reason. We all get tired and say foolish things. I have more respect for Senator Goldwater than to think he meant that."

The motorcade downtown moved fast and was ignored by the good people of New York. At the corner of Madison Avenue and Fifty-second Street, the candidate climbed up on a shaky table on the sidewalk outside a Democratic headquarters, and within a few minutes he had rounded up a lunch-hour crowd that blocked the cross street, irritating several cabdrivers considerably. While they shouted and honked, he orated about the negativism of Barry Goldwater.

While most members of Congress were working constructively on legislation, he said, Senator Goldwater always could be seen "sitting under the No-No tree in the shade of his own indifference. . . . I have said a number of times about Mr. Goldwater that I consider him to be a loyal, patriotic American. I have never made a personal comment about him in terms of his fine family or himself, and I don't think one needs to. It isn't his private life, it is his public utterances that disturb me. I happen to think that Mr. Goldwater would make a wonderful neighbor—but a very poor President. . . . Now, I want you to know that I have been highly honored in this campaign. I never knew that anybody took quite so much interest in who was going to be Vice-President. But for all of you that may be concerned, the candidate for President is Lyndon Johnson, and when you elect him, like it or not, you get me, too. So I suppose the opposition has a point. They say you ought to take a look at that Humphrey. Well, look me over, folks. I feel fine. . . ."

He outshouted the traffic noises and entertained his audience until he was ready to quit, which was not for some time. Then he went off to the Waldorf-Astoria to let some big Democratic contributors look him over at a private luncheon. Afterward, Walter Cronkite came by for an interview at the hotel, and the yelling street orator was soft-spoken, precise and knowledgeable beyond the limits of most ordinary mortals' curiosity.

At Charleston, two and a half hours later, Humphrey entered the barnlike Civic Center and walked through the stomping, cheering audience to the platform. The advance man's schedule, prepared for the crew handling the paid television broadcast, said, "Senator Humphrey enters hall and makes way through crowd to platform. Pandemonium reigns. TV cameras pan ecstatic throng." It was not quite pandemonium and the people were not quite ecstatic, but they were glad to see him. In his speech he recalled his campaign in the West Virginia Presidential primary of 1960, when he lost to John F. Kennedy. "You made the right choice," he said, "and I thank the people of West Virginia for your good judgment."

Toward the end of his prepared address, Humphrey said, "This is the question each American must ask before voting on November third: whose finger do I want on the nuclear trigger?" Throughout the campaign Humphrey used the finger on the trigger and Mr. Johnson used the thumb on the button; it was a fundamental difference in style, but it carried the message either way.

As the television time came to an end, with the frantic young director bouncing on the camera platform in front of the rostrum and signaling desperately to Humphrey with a cutting motion at the throat, it was obvious that the candidate was not nearly finished. He hit a good strong line with ten seconds left, drew a big round of applause for the fade-out, and went right on talking until he had said all he wanted to say.

In Cincinnati, a few minutes after ten o'clock, he spoke to a Democratic banquet in the Sheraton-Gibson Hotel. At the top of his form he was a spellbinder with a rapid-fire style that was always controlled, rhythmic, and perfectly attuned to the audience, and he was at the top of his form in Cincinnati. "I say that Senator Goldwater has disqualified himself from the Presidency," he told the enthralled Democrats, some of whom had been showing signs a few minutes earlier of dozing a little after drinks and a good dinner. "I say that he is a radical, if you please, a radical in every sense of the word. . . . By its refusal to condemn the lunatic fringe of American politics, the Goldwater party has welcomed to its ranks those whose stock in trade is the politics of hate. For a generation these extremists and radicals have been pushing their filth and their accusations in the back alleys of American politics.

Now they have come off the street corners and are peddling their hideous wares in the front parlors of what was once a proud and honored establishment."

Now as "The Happy Warrior" descended upon Lexington, Kentucky, at twelve-thirty A.M., most members of the traveling party were asleep or staring groggily at the ceiling. When the plane touched down, Humphrey came brightly and briskly out of his compartment at the rear, banging the backs of friends and saying that he only regretted he could not make three or four more speeches before he went to bed. Anyone could have said it; only Hubert Humphrey could have meant it.

Two thousand people, predominantly students from the University of Kentucky, were waiting for him in front of the terminal at this unholy hour on a drizzly night. "Democrats have the kind of vitality that makes them want to carry on at this hour," he said. "I don't think you live long this way, but it's sure fun while you're living." A lone heckler perched on the roof of the terminal sounded a halfhearted boo, and Humphrey thanked him for staying up so that everything would seem natural. He told some stories about his uncle, a black sheep who persisted in embarrassing the family by voting Republican, and soon everyone was laughing, including the heckler. It was the giddy laughter of the weary celebrants of a strange rite—the same laughter you could hear when you were walking through the rain and the mobs with the President, or when Vic Gold was screeching and flapping his arms at a bus driver who had lost Senator Goldwater in the side streets of nowhere.

On Thursday, October 29, five days before the election, Barry Goldwater meandered across southern Pennsylvania on a train, speaking in bleak railroad yards to small crowds on a gray day. Most of the people who turned out to see Goldwater in Harrisburg, Lewistown, Huntingdon, Altoona, Johnstown and Greensburg were devoted to him, but he still dealt with them like a man keeping appointments with strangers. The President would have charged at them, embraced them, cajoled and lectured them; Goldwater was polite, shy, friendly in a distant way.

He spoke at Harrisburg early in the morning from a makeshift platform on an overpass, with the crowd in the street far below him. "Well, this will be our last tour through Pennsylvania as a candidate. Our next tour will be as President," he said. He said it quietly, matter-of-factly. The crowd had not expected this casual prediction, and there seemed to be a gasp before the cheer. "Last night, just before I went to bed, I heard somebody say on television that I had just about given up. Well, I have news for him: this is going to be the greatest political upset of this century. Millions of unhappy, disgusted Americans will see to that."

As the train rolled toward Lewistown, a Goldwater staff man looked out the window at the Juniata River, a clear, placid stream with faded autumn foliage arching over its banks. He was very tired. Yes, he would have to agree that the candidate's schedule for this last week was somewhat unusual by the prior standards of Presidential campaigning. The Goldwater entourage had spent the first part of the week in places like Salisbury, Maryland; Dover, Delaware; London, Kentucky; Cedar Rapids, Iowa; and Oshkosh, Wisconsin—all fine places, no doubt, but hardly centers of population. A trip to Miami and other cities in Florida, where the Republican chances were considered good, had been canceled. The candidate had spent the previous night in a Harrisburg hotel —no speech. He just took the night off. Now he was visiting small cities in Pennsylvania, a state he was considered almost sure to lose. "I don't have anything to do with the schedule," the staff man said. "A committee handles it, a committee. I don't know what the committee is thinking about." Then he turned away from the window and said, "I like this man. I wish it had gone better for him."

Lewistown was drab, and there were perhaps a thousand people there. While the candidate walked to a nearby platform to speak, Denison Kitchel, his lawyer friend from Arizona, the amateur who was managing his campaign, stood pensively on the tracks at the rear of the train, staring down at the cinders. Goldwater talked about Social Security; he was not against it, he was for it, and he thought the people of Lewistown ought to know that his position had been misrepresented. It was New Hampshire nine months ago, all over again. It had always been the same.

The crowds were better in Huntingdon and Altoona, and the candidate talked about "Landslide Lyndon" and the mysteries of vote counting in Texas. He was not a fiery prosecutor, however; he joked about vote counting in Texas. His words were tougher but his delivery was bland when he came to Social Security: "I have voted for every improvement in Social Security since I have been in the Senate . . . and I promised on the floor of the Senate that should it ever come to a vote—and it didn't—I would vote for this year's amendments . . . which would have meant more money to every one of you in this audience and within the sound of my voice if it had passed. But it didn't, and do you know why? Lyndon Johnson killed those amendments because he couldn't get attached to it his Medicare plan, which nobody in the Congress wanted. . . . Because the President couldn't get his way, his selfish way on a measure that, so help me, I haven't found anybody that wants it yet, a measure that is as phony as a three-dollar bill, he just said to the boys, 'Turn it off'—and you can hear the bones crunch and the skin go and the heads banged together, and you recipients of Social Security aren't getting more today because of President Johnson.

I promise you that Goldwater had nothing to do with it. That Texan had the whole blame."

West of Altoona, the train turned the big horseshoe curve on the Pennsylvania Railroad high in the Alleghenies, slipped under the crest of the mountains in a tunnel, and rumbled down into the valley toward Johnstown. The press staff passed out the text of the speech that the candidate would deliver at a rally in Pittsburgh that night. Whole pages of it had been lifted from the speech he had made in Cleveland a few nights earlier. Goldwater spoke in Johnstown in front of the station, which was far below the trestle where the train stopped. He had a small but enthusiastic crowd that liked his speech. He was interrupted by a train of forty-eight cattle cars moving very slowly and rattling very loud on the trestle.

"Well," the candidate said after the long wait, "there were more cows in that train than there are in the whole state of Arizona. You know, Lyndon will do anything to keep me from talking. He just waved to me from the caboose on his way out."

At Greensburg, a town of 18,000 near Pittsburgh, Goldwater found 2,000 people in the courtyard of a charming old Tudor railroad station. There was a grassy bank on one side, and trees, and the crowd seemed to be in a remarkably friendly, cheerful humor, although the drizzle was turning into a steady rain. When the Senator was introduced, a large knot of college- and high-school-age spectators suddenly lifted a little forest of "LBJ" signs and waved them vigorously. Now the atmosphere was not so pleasant. There had been a few heckling incidents during the day—nothing like those the President had been involved in recently, but incidents that obviously unsettled Senator Goldwater. Throughout the campaign he had found it hard not to show his resentment of chanting, yowling youngsters, particularly when his wife was

with him. Mrs. Goldwater was with him now, sitting somewhat tensely at the back of the platform in the courtyard.

These young people did not chant or yowl; they just waved
their "LBJ" signs. Senator Goldwater looked at them appre-
hensively and began his speech in a low key. With his first
words, the signs went down. When he ventured some fairly
sharp criticisms of the President, the LBJ faction remained
quiet and the signs stayed out of sight. When he finished his
speech, all the signs waved again, but there were no boos.

He stepped back to the microphones, and the signs went
down again. "I want to say a word to our young friends over
here," he said. "You are opposed to me, I know, but you have
been gentlemanly about it. That is the American way—the
only way we can get our story across. I thank you for it." The
LBJ faction began to applaud. The rest of the crowd, after a
moment, took it up.

"I want you to know," Goldwater said, "that I've argued
with Lyndon Johnson and we've snapped at each other in the
Senate, in his office and in my office, but we can still call
each other friends."

Maybe so, maybe not, but the crowd applauded the idea. It
had been a harsh campaign and it had gone on too long. For
a while there in the courtyard of the railroad station at
Greensburg, Pennsylvania, anyway, everyone felt better about
everything and the sky was not falling after all.

On Election Day, November 3, the voting began at 12:01
A.M., Eastern Standard Time, when the polls opened in several eager-beaver New England towns, and it ended 26 hours
later when the polls closed in Alaska.

During the day I opened an envelope that had been lying
around for a couple of days, and it turned out to contain a
press release from the national headquarters of the Citizens'
Councils of America in Jackson, Mississippi. It said: "While
the Citizens' Councils of America has never endorsed any
candidate for political office, and does not now do so, we feel
that our members and friends throughout the nation will be
interested in knowing the results of a confidential pre-elec-
tion survey which we have conducted. Reports from our
leaders, field workers and other reliable political sources in
every part of the country indicate that a record number of
white Americans will vote for Senator Goldwater on Tuesday. Our survey shows that Senator Goldwater is leading in
states with a minimum of 277 electoral votes—or seven more
than the number necessary for victory. The survey rates the

election as a toss-up in states with another 128 electoral votes. Thus, if the trend of the past two weeks continues, Senator Goldwater's total could well run as high as 405 electoral votes, making his victory a landslide of major proportions."

Most of the other polls and surveys did not see it that way. They predicted that President Johnson would receive 60 per cent or more of the popular vote and carry most of the states. There was nothing to do but wait for the television broadcasters and their marvelous machinery to tell us what was happening.

At 6:29 P.M., NBC said that Mr. Johnson had carried Kentucky, and 20 minutes later the network's marvelous machinery, brooding over the scattered returns from a few other states, said that Mr. Johnson would win the election with more than 60 per cent of the vote. The other networks' machines said that was how it looked to them, too.

At 7:19 P.M., Roger Mudd and Harry Reasoner on CBS gave Connecticut and Maryland to Mr. Johnson, and a minute later David Brinkley on NBC said Mr. Johnson was ahead in Tennessee but Senator Goldwater had the lead in South Carolina. Chet Huntley talked with a machine and came away with the impression that Indiana had gone for Mr. Johnson. Walter Cronkite gave Mississippi to Goldwater at 7:22. Howard K. Smith and Edward P. Morgan on ABC noted at 7:30 that Mr. Johnson was a million votes ahead in Ohio, and that meant to them a "massive Democratic victory" all over the country.

In the next few minutes Hughes Rudd on CBS found some backlash in Chicago but not enough for Senator Goldwater to take heart about Illinois, although he carried Alabama. Mr. Johnson carried North Carolina. He also carried Vermont at 7:42, and that struck men and machines alike as an event of considerable moment.

At 8:02, David Brinkley reminded everyone to go and vote

if the polls had not yet closed in their states. The polls had not closed, as a matter of fact, in New York and many states to the west, but the result certainly had been obvious since Vermont toppled, or even since the backlashers had not lashed very hard in Chicago and Maryland.

Goldwater carried Georgia on ABC at 8:29, but CBS gave Virginia to Mr. Johnson at 8:35. The CBS machinery said at a few minutes after 9 o'clock that Michigan and Florida had gone Democratic, and everybody's machinery agreed by 9:30 that Mr. Johnson had won by a landslide. At 9:44, the President showed up shaking hands diligently outside the Driskill Hotel in Austin, Texas. Senator Goldwater was in his house in Phoenix with a few friends and no television cameras.

Through the evening, the President continued to win state after state by big margins. Large numbers of Republican candidates for the House, the Senate and governorships were going down with Senator Goldwater. By 11:45, all the network newsmen, supported by their machinery, were using words like "debacle" to describe the Republican situation. A few people were looking around halfheartedly for the tide of conservative sentiment that had been discussed so much at the beginning of the campaign, but it was a hard tide to find. Mr. Johnson came on, shaking hands in Austin again, and said to Cronkite in New York, "We are all thinking of you, Walter." The President was not claiming victory, because that would not be protocol until Senator Goldwater conceded it. The Senator was going to bed in Phoenix without conceding anything.

By midnight the machines were more or less agreed that Mr. Johnson would receive more than 42,000,000 votes (the most in history), that he would win by a margin of more than 15,000,000 votes (the largest margin in history), and that he would wind up with 486 electoral votes to Goldwater's 47 (the largest electoral-vote landslide except for

Franklin D. Roosevelt's in 1936, when he held Alfred M. Landon to 8). Goldwater would win a belt of 5 Deep South states—South Carolina, Georgia, Alabama, Mississippi and Louisiana—and his home state of Arizona, where the contest was very close.

At 12:04 A.M., Governor George Romney of Michigan came on television. He had won his race for re-election while Mr. Johnson was sweeping his state by a tremendous majority, and a Republican who could do that was a man to be reckoned with. Within minutes everyone was reckoning with him—wondering how he and Governor Scranton and Governor Rockefeller and Representative Lindsay and Richard Nixon would fare in the maneuvering for the nomination in 1968.

It was over, and it was beginning again.

DATE DUE

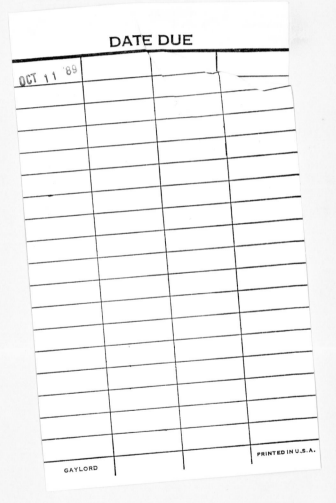

OCT 11 '89

GAYLORD

PRINTED IN U.S.A.